elisabeth
klein
corcoran

unraveling

hanging on to
faith through
the end of a
Christian marriage

Abingdon Press
NASHVILLE

UNRAVELING
HANGING ON TO FAITH THROUGH THE END OF A CHRISTIAN MARRIAGE

Copyright © 2013 by Elisabeth Klein Corcoran

Library of Congress Cataloging-in-Publication Data

Corcoran, Elisabeth K., 1970-
 Unraveling : hanging onto faith through the end of a Christian marriage / Elisabeth Klein Corcoran.
  pages cm
  ISBN 978-1-4267-7027-2 (book - pbk. / trade pbk./binding: soft black : alk. paper)
 1. Divorce—Religious aspects—Christianity. 2. Marriage—Religious aspects—Christianity I. Title.
 BT707.C67 2013
 248.8'46—dc23   2013018358

13 14 15 16 17 18 19 20 21 22—10 9 8 7 6 5 4 3 2 1

MANUFACTURED IN THE UNITED STATES OF AMERICA

Contents

Contents

Contents

*U*nraveling is dedicated to each of the women in my private Facebook groups for courageously sharing their stories with me. I wrote this for you. We are not alone.

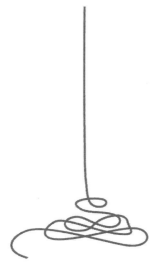

Introduction

What you're holding in your hands is a narrative of my journey through the most difficult, confusing, and emotional season of my entire life. It is the chronicling of me bottoming out and then finding I wasn't alone when I reached my end. It is the chronicling of battling every fear and every sadness and every judgment and then realizing there was hope and light and joy waiting for me. And it is the chronicling of not knowing if I was following God's leading or walking away and then finding out that he was right there, as close as a breath, following through on his promise to never abandon me, no matter what.

So although this is not the story of my marriage nor the story of my divorce, I do believe you deserve a brief background.

I was married for almost nineteen years. During that time, my family and I attended a wonderful church that I loved and where I even held a staff position for several years. I am so grateful for the pastors and other people who served in leadership there. Around year sixteen of my marriage, I asked our church leadership to try to help me in my faltering marriage. For the next fifteen months, a group of godly people from my church—which included one pastor, one older couple, one mentoring couple, one female mentor, one counselor, and one mediator—tried, formally, to help my husband and me reconcile. My separation officially began with my husband moving out of our home. At the end of the fifteen-month reconciliation attempt, with great sadness, my pastor and church leadership agreed that legal separation was my next logical step, if I so chose, which I did pursue. The process of divorce began when I was served divorce papers. My children and I moved into a new home several months later. The divorce became final one year after the papers were served.

What led up to that and all the details that came in between are known by God, my ex-husband, myself, and the friends and family who came around us. My marriage was very difficult, and my divorce has been very difficult. But this isn't the place for those details, and I'll tell you why.

Because you, dear one, are living out your own story. My details might actually blur things for you. And because I am proclaiming—for the sake of your healing process and for the sake of falling lavishly on the side of grace—that I do not care how you came to find yourself separated or divorced, and therefore my specifics do not matter. What matters is the foundational truth that even in the most heartbreaking, soul-wrenching divorce, you, and I, can find peace, healing, and resurrection.

But to be clear, there are several things you should know about what I believe.

I believe in God, and I am a Christian. I accepted Christ into my heart and life when I was fifteen, and I try to follow him every day.

I believe the Bible is God's divinely inspired word to us.

I am 100 percent pro-marriage.

I believe God created marriage as a covenant to last for the lifetime of the couple.

I believe God created marriage as a breathtaking picture of how Christ loves his church.

I believe God allows marriages to end when certain sins are committed.

I believe the church is in place to protect and guide individuals and families through dark, confusing situations.

I believe God would have wanted my marriage to become healthy and remain intact.

I believe all marriages can be saved.

Yet, I believe God gives us free will.

I believe no one should walk away from their marriage without first getting as much help as they possibly can and trying their absolute hardest to keep it together.

I believe God is bringing about a different kind of miracle in my family—one of healing and resurrection and joy on the other side, and reaching out to others with the comfort we have received.

And I believe, when it all comes down, only you and God can know what you need to do.

Before we jump in, let me encourage you to feel every single feeling that you're experiencing. You must remember that you are grieving a significant loss, regardless of how you came to this point. Now is the time for the deeper works of resting and healing. Do not rush yourself through this process or through this book.

A brief note about the order of this book: you may notice in glancing at the table of contents that I talk about hope early on, for instance, and brokenness and exhaustion later, with happiness somewhere in the middle. The reason is this: although I am following a chronology of sorts as it pertains to my story, I have felt a hundred emotions in one day, and my divorce journey has not followed a straightforward path of anger, then sadness, then healing, then joy. It has been every feeling, every day, for the past few years. There is no clean-cut story arc, which is actually just how a crisis would play out, just like life. Also, the little snippets you'll find between each chapter come straight from my journals as I pull back the veil a bit more into how I truly felt while walking through all this.

And finally, before you begin, I want you to do me a favor. Put the book down, close your eyes, and say the following out loud:

God, I am precious and honored in your sight.
You love me no matter what.

Now repeat this mantra as often as you need to as you let God walk you through this unraveling season. Let him walk you through your unraveling. And let him begin the work of putting you back together again.

I think I'm doing everything wrong.

Raw

Prom my journal, on a random day of being separated:

*I am in a raw place today. I am swimming in the icy cold
waters of defeat, but the worst part is that my emotions are
numb and I am now used to this temperature. The water
doesn't feel icy anymore. It feels like home. It feels like the
water has caught me by the shoulders and is looking me in
the eyes and is making sure it has my full attention to tell
me, "You're not going anywhere—you belong here in this
dark place. This is just where you should be, and you do not
deserve for this to ever end. Get used to the cold; get used
to the dark. Say good-bye to the possibility of ever being
loved, of ever really loving."*

I cannot stand what I am feeling today. In part, because I have felt this way on so many of my days over the past twenty years. It is a swirling deep inside that I can't stop. My reality today is that I feel like I am trapped in partnership with someone who cannot stand me, and I feel that I am not allowed to sever this crumbling relationship without being ostracized in my community and, worse, without losing the favor of my loving heavenly Father.

So yes, I feel trapped today. I am breathing shallow breaths. And I am not seeing even one sliver of light at the end of this tunnel that is constricting around me. And I am lonely. And I am bitter. And I am angry. And I want to run away and never come back. And I am cold.

OK, so I just laid myself open for you, all vulnerable and open and leaving no feeling unsaid. Can I just say how completely freeing that was? I have kept these thoughts inside me for more than fifteen years. In other words, for most of my adult life, I have acted differently than I have felt. How heartbreaking.

Dear friend, I know I don't know you. And I don't wish to presume that our situations are identical, because I know that they are not. But I know that if you love Jesus and if you have been in a difficult marriage, those two things seem diametrically opposed. I know that you have probably felt emotions that were the complete opposite of what you thought you were *supposed* to be feeling, maybe for a very long time. And when you keep something like that to yourself, and when you allow it to finally see the light of day, *raw* is the only word to describe it.

No one likes to feel like this: exposed, defenseless, emotionally naked. But once you have gotten to this place of being able to speak your truest feelings, maybe after all these years, you will be ready to begin to be healed. God won't bother trying to paint over your pretenses. Instead, God will put forth amazing amounts of effort to take your wide-open, unguarded self and recover you, rebuild you, restore you. He can heal those emotions that feel so horrible and blackened and unspeakable. Do not be afraid. God is right there with you, able to handle whatever it is you've got buried deep inside.

A Prayer

Father, please enter in to my rawest places. I cannot even believe I feel the way I feel sometimes. I feel broken by my circumstances, and if I'm completely honest, maybe a bit abandoned by you. But I am choosing to believe that you're with me as you say you are, and I am choosing to trust that you want to bring me full healing. Amen.

A Next Good Step

Be honest with yourself. Stop acting as if everything is OK when it's not. If you're a mess, let yourself be a mess. If you need to yell, go sit in your car and yell as loud as you need to. If you need to cry, hide yourself in your bathroom and sob until the tears run dry. If you need to put words to feelings, journal it out or find a friend you can trust. But don't hold it in;

do not pretend. Simply push through your fear of what's inside and get it all out.

A Way Forward

You get us ready for life:

>   you probe for our soft spots,
>
>   you knock off our rough edges.

And I'm feeling so fit, so safe:

>   made right, kept right.

(Psalm 7:9 *THE MESSAGE*)

Hope

Several years ago, I knew someone who found out she was pregnant after much trying and waiting. She was deeply troubled to learn, then, that the pregnancy was ectopic, meaning that the egg had implanted somewhere other than in the uterus. Most ectopic pregnancies are not viable. The news was grim, and she was devastated. She had a friend, however, who told her she had a dream that my friend would have this baby, that it was a boy, and what she would name him. This expectant mother quickly turned ecstatic, newly convinced that God would bring a miracle healing. I remember one intense phone call where I gently tried to talk her down off that slippery ledge.

"Yes, God can do anything, but we just don't know if he will. Please hope in *him*, not in this baby being OK," I pleaded with her.

She miscarried. She was undone. And I think it's safe to say that something in her faith in God shifted after all of that.

I tell you this story because, although I don't know in detail what you are currently experiencing, I am currently being told left and right to have hope. To believe God for my marriage. To not despair. I, in part, understand where these well-meaning people are coming from: from a place where *they* want to have hope, *they* want to believe God for my marriage, and *they* do not want to despair. But I also think they don't want to have to deal with the discomfort that God may not heal us.

But the reality is he may not.

People who love Jesus and are trying to follow him with pure hearts get cancer and die, go to Iraq and die, have car accidents and die. We are not promised a bed of roses down here; in fact, there is nowhere in Scripture (that I have found—and trust me, I've looked) that promises all will be made well down here, right now, on this side of heaven.

I've heard Beth Moore put it this way: "Make no mistake . . . we have a Deliverer. He will either deliver us from suffering, deliver us through suffering, or deliver us on Home."

I needed a readjusting of my perception of hope, so I looked to Scripture: "Though he slay me, yet I will trust him" (Job 13:15).

We are to hope in God no matter what he does or does not do. "Yet when I hoped for good, evil came; / when I looked for light, then came darkness" (Job 30:26 NIV).

Don't hope in anything but God. "Sustain me according to your word so I can live! / Don't let me be put to shame because of hope" (Psalm 119:116).

God's promise is that he'll be there for me and sustain me, not that he'll answer me any way I want him to. And apparently, I can ask God to not allow my hope to fade. "Hopes placed in mortals die with them; all the promise of their power comes to nothing" (Proverbs 11:7 NIV).

I should not place my hope in a person.

We longed for relief,
        but received none;
for a time of healing,
        but found only terror.
(Jeremiah 8:15)

I should not hope for a certain outcome.

"Therefore, once you have your minds ready for action and you are thinking clearly, place your hope completely on the grace that will be brought to you when Jesus Christ is revealed" (1 Peter 1:13).

I have a bigger Hope.

I do not believe I have lost capital-H hope. I may have lost hope in my marriage, after years of seeing the same things over and over again; but I have not lost Hope in the one and only thing we're called to hope in, and that's God.

I still believe God can do absolutely anything. I've seen him do miracles. But I am not claiming any false promises of what he may do in my life's circumstances, because all he guarantees is that he'll get me through it and it will be for his glory, not that I'll love what he chooses to do or that it will be my idea of a miracle. So, sweet one, hope all you want; just make sure you are hoping on God and on nothing else.

A Prayer

We put our hope in you, Lord. You are our help and our shield. Our heart rejoices in you, God, because we trust your holy name. Lord, let your faithful love surround us, because we wait for you. Amen. —based on Psalm 33:20-22

A Next Good Step

Write a note to someone who is hurting today, and remind them of the hope they have in Christ.

A Way Forward

Why, I ask myself, are you so depressed?

Why are you so upset inside?

Hope in God!

Because I will again give him thanks,

my saving presence and my God. (Psalm 42:11)

I'm ashamed to say that
I sometimes want to
hurt him on purpose.
But I havent, and I wont.

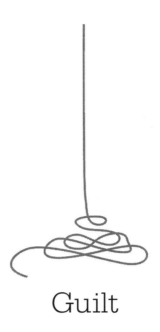

Guilt

I feel guilty that my marriage has failed. I feel guilty that maybe I didn't try hard enough to love my husband along the way. I feel guilty that I didn't pray hard enough, serve him often enough, respect him well enough all those years. I feel guilty that I didn't make sure we received proper help earlier on, even though I did ask. I feel guilty that I'm replicating my childhood in my own children's lives. I feel guilty that I haven't been able to reconcile with my husband. I feel guilty that I no longer want to. I feel guilty that I'm pretty much a single parent right now, and I'm afraid huge things are falling through the cracks with my kids. I feel guilty that, because of me, there isn't a man living in the house with them. I feel guilty that I hired someone to plow us out of a recent blizzard. I feel guilty that I've watched four movies in five days. I feel guilty that if I drink a smoothie and eat some dark chocolate, I feel pretty good about my health for the day. I feel guilty that I don't make a home-cooked meal for my kids every night of the week. (Umm, who am I kidding? *Most* nights of the week.) I feel guilty that I don't leave my house each day and drive to a "real job." I feel guilty that I'm not volunteering. I feel guilty that I want to sleep in every day. I feel guilty when I actually do sleep in. I feel guilty if I snap at one of my kids. I feel guilty if I don't take them to task on something because I don't want them mad at me right now. I feel guilty that I'm not a hugely invested, outward-focused friend these days.

Most of all, I feel guilty because I feel like I'm in sin—being separated and divorcing—while, at the same time, I feel like I'm not. But then again, I sort of do. And yet, I don't.

Here's why I feel *in sin* right now. Because I am supposed to have enough strength in Christ to get along with everyone, especially the person I took a vow to get along with the most. Because some people have made it quite clear that they believe my husband should be back in our home, and that he is not back here, in their opinion, because of me. Because it says in the Bible, "Do not separate." (Thank God that it goes on to say, "but if you do . . ." because that implies that some people clearly will.) Because even though I have received wise counsel and read myriad books that tell me sometimes separation is the best thing for a broken relationship, it can still feel scandalous and controversial and just plain wrong.

I am going through the book of Philippians with a dear friend. I'm writing out verses that jump out at me, and little thoughts that come up, and then we talk about them together. Here's what I shared with my friend just this morning: "If you've gotten anything at all out of following Christ . . . then . . . agree with each other, love each other" (Philippians 2:1-2 *THE MESSAGE*). And I said to her, "This is guilt upon guilt for me. I have gotten *everything* out of following Christ. So, what does it mean that I am clearly failing at agreeing with someone, failing at loving someone? I can't stand that loving God and loving my husband seem so intrinsically bound. Will I forever be in sin because I cannot love this man?" I looked at her and shrugged with resignation and a sigh.

Then my dear friend said, "Maybe just read to read. Don't look at everything through the eyes of your current circumstances. I'm not saying don't apply it because that's what we're supposed to do, but maybe for now just read it as Beth." Then she added a little disclaimer, "But what do I know?"

"You know a lot," I told her.

So that's what I'm going to try. For a little while at least. I'm just going to read to read.

And today I open my Bible and my eyes fall on this: "There is therefore now no condemnation for those who are in Christ Jesus" (Romans 8:1 ESV). And I am reminded that Christ did not die on the cross so that we would continue to carry all of this around with us. He came to take the weight of the world off our shoulders, so today, I'm going to let him.

A Prayer

"Lord, in your mercy, forgive all our sins against one another. Take from our hearts all suspicion, hard feelings, anger, dissension, and whatever else may diminish the love we could have for one another. Have mercy, O Lord, on all who ask for your mercy. Give grace to all who need it." —Thomas à Kempis, from *A Forgiving Heart: Prayers for Blessing and Reconciliation*

A Next Good Step

List all of your current sins, all that you are feeling guilty for; ask Christ's forgiveness; then burn or shred that list and breathe in his freedom.

A Way Forward

"But if we confess our sins, he is faithful and just to forgive us our sins and cleanse us from everything we've done wrong." (1 John 1:9)

I feel like I've got nothin' lately—no life, no spark, no light. Nothing.

Heart

I have a hard heart. My heart is hard and cold and wounded and tired and done. Not hard to God. Not cold toward my family or friends. But closed off to the one I once loved most.

At the time of this writing, it is the beginning of the Lenten season. I view Lent as preparation. As giving something up. As laying something down—something of value to you. Something that takes up your thoughts and your time and your energy. Something that may even be good but isn't the best. Something that moves your thoughts and your time and your energy away from the Source of Life and Love. And, in preparation, we could replace those empty spaces with thoughts and time and energy that focus on the Resurrection of Life and Love.

I haven't given something up for Lent in years. I wasn't planning on giving anything up this year either. But what's forty days in the scheme of things?

In my specific life circumstances, forty days did not just bring me to Easter. It brought me to the six-week point after a benchmark meeting. A meeting where a gauntlet was thrown down by our church leaders, for me and for my husband. I had asked our church leadership for help with our marriage, and they had stepped in. Months into our separation, we both had several things to work on within ourselves to be made whole.

But when it all came down, *my main task was this: be ready if he tries to win your heart back.*

There is not one thing I can control regarding my husband's thoughts toward me, his intentions toward me, his words or actions toward me. But I am in control of the state of my heart—at least, I am told that I am.

So we were both told, one final time, to do what we were supposed to have been doing all along: my husband, pursue me; me, receive any pursuing.

It did occur to me, what is the worst thing that can happen? I open my heart, I begin to want my husband back, I begin to long for him again, and my heart gets broken one more time? Oh well. Then God will just have to heal my heart yet again. He's done it before, he can do it again if need be.

So for the next forty days, each single day, for the purpose of being obedient to God and looking for Christ in everything, I am giving up my hard heart for Lent. It began with the idea of simply saying to God something like, "Here is my heart, Lord. Please take it and change it," each morning during my devotions. Then I ratcheted it up a bit, once I realized that my thoughts were wandering and going haywire a thousand times each day. I decided to take those errant thoughts captive, and each time a cynical thought about my marriage slithered through my mind, I would say out loud, "I'm sorry, Lord. My sin was enough on its own that you had to die. I am a sinner. Please change my heart of stone into a heart of flesh."

Ahh, but then entered friendship. I have women surrounding me who love me, who challenge me. And one dear friend suggested I up the ante even more. She suggested I take my love of rituals and create a moment that would allow me to look back and remember that I have laid my hard heart down once and for all.

So this morning, I found a stone from my beach collection and wrote on one side: "my hard heart toward my husband." On the other side I wrote: "Surrender. Ezekiel 11:19." I walked out to the pond that is attached to our property— that I can see from my office desk and from my living room— and I waded through spider webs and bramble and thistles and mud. I found a spot at water's edge, and with the weight of the cold rock in my palm, I held it up to God and looked at the sky. I told him that this was a symbol of my hard heart, that I had become so used to it as a comfort and as security and as protection, but that I wanted to be free. I then confessed that I wasn't ready to give it up fully but acknowledged that this was a start. I hiked my arm back and flung it as far as I could, hearing the *splish* and watching the ripples as it sank to the bottom and the sludge. I walked away, thanking him for the process of replacing my heart of stone with a heart of flesh.

I stepped into my house and grabbed the laundry, feeling quite the same. But then I looked out my window to the pond and said, to no one in particular, "My hard heart is out there now." And my heart will rest and watch and wait for God. No matter what happens.

A Prayer

God, my heart is in quite the state. Your word says that my heart can be deceitful above all things. My heart can be evil, it can be troubled, it can be drawn to things it shouldn't be drawn to. It can be hardened, broken, led astray, unyielding. But my heart can also prompt, it can be moved, store your word, be inclined to you, and love you with its whole being. I believe that you know my heart better than I do, so I lay it before you in whatever condition you find it in this moment. It's yours. Do as you please. Amen.

A Next Good Step

Maybe you need to create a ritual for yourself. Maybe you have unforgiveness or bitterness or fear lurking in your heart today. Consider finding a stone, writing your key word on it, and burying it or tossing it into a field or lake.

A Way Forward

"Even if our hearts condemn us, God is greater than our hearts and knows all things." (1 John 3:20)

Tired. So tired. Want to crawl right back into bed. Again.

Opinions

When I was a very little girl, I didn't care what anybody thought of me. It didn't even cross my mind that not everyone in the world loved me. Then I hit, I don't know, maybe second grade. Suddenly, my Garanimals didn't always match and I was pigeon-toed and kids could be cruel, and I realized that not everyone loved me or even liked me. I started to care what people thought. I carried that with me all the way through junior high and high school and into college, trying to fit in or at least not be noticed, whichever was less painful. I thought that feeling would fall away with adulthood and maturity, but it just got quieter and more suppressed. And the categories of comparison changed.

I compared myself with friends who were married already, then friends who already had babies, then friends who had big houses, then how much leadership responsibility so-and-so was given at church, then how many books so-and-so sold, and on and on it went. Now, I don't even think I realized I was doing this . . . this comparison game, this wondering what others thought of me or how much I was liked or not liked. . . . I just did it.

In fact, it wasn't until I gave a talk at my church several years ago where I revealed some of my more personal struggles that it even occurred to me that there might be people who compared themselves to me. A gal came up to me and said, "Until tonight, I thought you had the perfect life . . . the perfect marriage, the perfect job, the perfect clothes, the perfect kids. . . . I don't think that anymore." Not sure how she meant that, but I took it as the ultimate compliment. I had let others in—to see my darkness and all, and it wasn't pretty but it was real.

Then somewhere around the time I quit my staff position at church, I decided that I didn't care what people thought of me anymore. I had based so much of my identity on my work at church, on succeeding or at least on people thinking I was a hard worker who covered her bases while loving Jesus. Then I just up and quit. Because I had wanted to. Because I was exhausted. Because I felt God tell me I could and that he'd still love me if I stopped. And for a thousand other reasons. I stopped caring what people thought of me, and it was freeing.

But then the pendulum swung and I started to care again. You see, I'm the goody-two-shoes. I'm the teacher's pet. I follow the rules. I do what I'm told. I hate disappointing people. I hate failing people. I hate letting people down. If someone doesn't like me or is mad at me, I'm undone. And I hate, hate, hate being talked about, being pondered over, being judged, being told that I'm wrong or in sin.

Don't get me wrong—I am all for the truth, and for truth being told to me in love. And I've got a great support system around me, people who are willing and who actually do that. Although it's hard, I'll take it, because I realize that they know me well and they love me through and through.

But it turns out, I don't like being told that I am sinning by being separated or getting divorced. Or even knowing that people *think* I'm sinning—when I honestly, down to my core, don't think that I am. That's when I super-care what people think about me.

I received an e-mail recently that sliced me open, and had I allowed myself to read it more than once, I would still be in bed with the curtains drawn. The e-mail, which came from a friend, was harsh and accusatory, not once taking into consideration my current vulnerability nor the fact that I was trying to do everything I was being told to do to fix my marriage. I felt completely unheard, completely judged and juried. And it broke something in me. It kills me that this person thinks these things about me. But I chose not to send a response. I chose not to defend myself, again, despite everything in me wanting to explain each accusation away.

And here's why. Although, of course, I don't wish for anyone to hate me or think ill of me, I really do need to care about only one opinion of me, and that's God's. God knows my heart better than I do, and certainly better than those who are looking on from a distance.

And so I sat down with my Bible and cried and said, very simply, "Jesus, how do you see me? Because you're the only one I really care about anyway." A certain psalm came to my mind instantly—I love when he does that, by the way—and I opened the pages of my Bible and read this:

Count yourself lucky, how happy you must be—
>   you get a fresh start,
>   your slate's wiped clean.
Count yourself lucky—
>   God holds nothing against you. . . .
(Psalm 32:1-2 *THE MESSAGE*)

God holds nothing against me. I gasped. Then tears ran down my cheeks. All I could think to say, over and over, was, "Thank you, Jesus . . . thank you, Jesus . . . I love you." Only one opinion counts, really. And his Truth washed over me, healing me a bit more and clearing out space for more of the same.

So finally I've come to rest in the middle. I knew I'd be OK when I recently ran into someone I used to go to church with but hadn't seen for years. I told her, someone who wasn't in my inner circle yet someone whose opinion I care about, that I was separated. I told her it wasn't for the typical black-and-white reasons. . . . I told her it was scandalous and controversial. We both laughed a bit but we both had tears in our eyes. And I realized that her tears were not of judgment but of concern and compassion. That's when I knew I'd be OK with whatever happened. That's when I knew I would be able to move forward with my head held high, no matter the outcome.

May we listen for only one voice . . . the only one that really matters . . . because that voice is Love.

A Prayer

Creator God, who do you say I am? What do I mean to you? Do you really love me, just as I am? Please speak to me deep down in my soul. I need to be reminded of your great love that's not contingent on anything else but your goodness. Amen.

A Next Good Step

Sit down with your Bible and ask Jesus what I asked Jesus: "How do you see me?" Then quiet your heart and listen, really listen, to what he says about you. And whatever you do, don't rail against his loving response.

A Way Forward

"I care very little if I am judged by you or by any human court; indeed, I do not even judge myself. My conscience is clear, but that does not make me innocent. It is the Lord who judges me." (1 Corinthians 4:3-4 NIV)

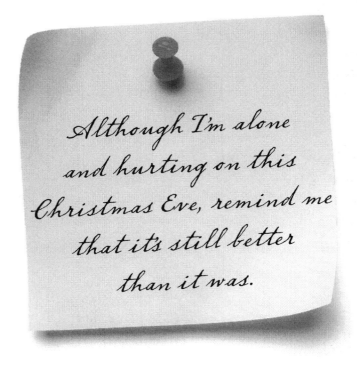

Although I'm alone and hurting on this Christmas Eve, remind me that it's still better than it was.

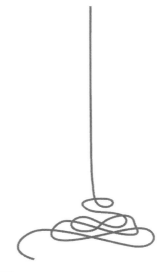

Perseverance

W inston Churchill once said, "Never, ever, ever, ever, ever, ever, ever give up. Never give up. Never give up. Never give up." There will be days that you feel like throwing in the towel—the towel of your marriage, the towel of your faith, the towel of your life. The separation of two human beings who were made into one is a unique kind of pain. It hollows you out. It leaves you cracked and dry and empty. It can feel, at times, unmendable, like you will never be whole again. This has been the largest, longest, most all-consuming, most fracturing pain of my life.

But I want to encourage you to not let the dark voices win. I am not telling you to persevere in your marriage at all costs. I cannot presume to understand the intricacies of your situation, nor do I know your heart. All I will tell you is this: stay as close to God as you can. And although I won't tell you one way or the other if you should stick it out or walk away regarding your marriage—because only God can tell you this—I will urge you to do whatever is required to walk this thing through with integrity. I don't know what your road of integrity looks like right now. Perhaps it means going to one more counseling session, even though you don't want to; or maybe it means standing firm in saying that the time for just one more counseling session has come and gone. It could mean reaching out to your spouse once more to suggest reconciliation; or it might mean clearly telling your spouse that it is time that you both moved on. The road of integrity is the longer, slower road, one filled with the uphill climb of words left unsaid, kindnesses shown in spite of ourselves and our pain, and boundaries held firmly but with grace. And yet it is the road that will allow you to move through this with your head held high. Don't give up on that road.

I will also tell you to not give up when it comes to your faith. God is committed to journeying beside you, to leading you, to guiding you. There will be quiet moments when it feels as if you're alone and God has up and left. I've been there. I've felt that. At times I've begged for the presence and the peace and instead felt silence and the cold shoulder. L. L. Barkat says, "Beyond the cross, we still experience Divine advance and retreat, presence and absence, light and darkness, union and separation. . . . The night is a season, not the whole, just a slice." But know this: God hasn't left you. The path you're walking with God may feel like the steeper one, the more dangerous one, but the views will be better along the way and the closer you'll have to walk with him to get through. Don't give up on God.

And do not give up on your hope of living a vital life. Your life may not feel vital right now—in fact, *you* may not feel all that vital right now—but don't close up shop. Don't draw the shades. Don't count yourself out of the game just yet, just on the bench for a little while. You're tired, but you're not finished. The enemy wants you to think you're damaged beyond repair, that God not only can't use you to be a light, but that he doesn't *want* to use you to be a light; that God himself is ashamed of you. Those are lies. If you're still breathing, if you are still holding on to God, there is still a plan with your name written on it; there are still plenty more of your stories to be told. It's OK if you move a little slower. It's OK if you need to be alone a bit more to refuel. But hold on to these truths: God wants to use you now, even in the middle of all of this mess. And God wants to use you later, after, when it's all said and done. Don't give up on your life.

Don't ever, ever, ever give up, sweet one.

A Prayer

"Gracious and holy Father, please give me: intellect to understand you; reason to discern you; diligence to seek you; wisdom to find you; a spirit to know you; a heart to meditate upon you; ears to hear you; eyes to see you; a tongue to proclaim you; a way of life pleasing to you; patience to wait for you; and perseverance to look for you. Grant me: a perfect end, your holy presence. A blessed resurrection, and life everlasting." —St. Benedict of Nursia (480–547)

A Next Good Step

Think of one thing that you feel like giving up on today. Write it on a scrap of paper and fold it up. On the other side of the paper, write, "I can keep doing this for one more day."

A Way Forward

"We are experiencing all kinds of trouble, but we aren't crushed. We are confused, but we aren't depressed. We are harassed, but we aren't abandoned. We are knocked down, but we aren't knocked out." (2 Corinthians 4:8-9)

Thanking you in advance for setting all things right . . . some day.

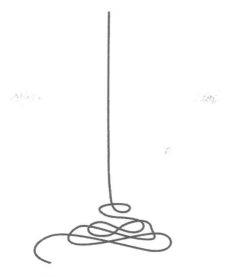

Flourishing

On my walk this morning, I was thinking about what I had read earlier in the day: "Those who plant with tears / reap the harvest with joyful shouts" (Psalm 126:5). I have long taken comfort in these words. I have taken them to mean that *I may be crying now, Lord, but you will bring me joy eventually*, which in and of itself is totally true. But it just hit me in a new way that there is an action involved. This is not an equation that says our tears today automatically equal joy later on. This is not a passive verse. These are not simply

words of comfort from a Master to his servant, from a Father
to his daughter. Although they are comforting words, these
are also fightin' words. These are words of challenge. This is
a battle cry, even to someone who is weary and worn down
and wants to stop walking the hard road, who would like to
stop walking altogether if given the chance.

Through these words, I believe God is saying to me:

*I know you're hurting, I know you want to stop. I know you
want to stay in your pajamas every day. And every once in
a while that is even OK. But don't just sit there and cry and
wait for the joy to magically appear, because it doesn't work
that way. Sow. Now. In the meantime. In the waiting. In the
unraveling. Sow seeds intermingled with your pain and
sadness. Walk through the sadness. Don't pretend you're
not sad, don't stuff it down. But don't remain paralyzed by
it either. And as you walk and move and live and breathe
deeply and laugh occasionally and serve, all amid your tears
and pain, you will eventually sow much, much deep joy.
Deeper joy than you'd experience if you just sat around and
cried and let time pass. Yes, there is pain and yes, you are
in it up to your neck. But sow, even if it's only in bits and
pieces and fits and starts; sow a little here into your children's lives, a little there into a friend's life, a little here into
your own soul, a little there into the life of someone who
might be hurting more than you.*

I received a fairly benign phone call the other day, but
because of where I'm at emotionally, it left me in tears. So I
called a friend to vent, and she listened and prayed for me and
then said, "Don't let the enemy steal the rest of this day from
you because of that conversation." So I didn't. I prayed for a
friend. I wrote a little bit. I cleaned out my linen closet. And
while I was deciding what to keep and what to throw away in

that mess of a closet that so resembled my life, it occurred to me that I am currently having to reinvent myself. I lost some speaking engagements when I announced my separation, which hurt deeply. I stepped down from the AIDS team I was leading at church in an effort to take things off my plate that might distract me from healing. Having to step down from some fairly public ministries and having to find new things to do that are quieter and in the background has been humbling.

One small thing I landed on is volunteering in the third grade class at my kids' school twice a month. It's ninety minutes when I do not think about me or my problems or my sadness. As we work on math facts, I'm thinking of someone other than me. As we prepare for a test, I'm sowing some seeds. It's a very small act of service and the little boy that I'm working with will more than likely not remember me by midsummer, but I'm choosing, in small ways, to sow. I'm still walking, I'm sowing in my tears, and I'm waiting to reap the promised joy.

A Prayer

"Holy Spirit of Christ, you have planned every detail of my life, every trial, every joy—all things to work together for my eternal purpose. Let my tears soften the soil as I sow in your service. God of all grace, restore me and establish the work of my hands, yes, establish the work of my hands. I pray in Jesus' name and for his glory. Amen." —Ann C. Schwiesow

A Next Good Step

What do you love to do? Find a way to use a hobby or talent to serve someone, even if for a half hour a week as a start. Then get dressed and get out of the house.

A Way Forward

"Make no mistake, God is not mocked. A person will harvest what they plant. Those who plant only for their own benefit will harvest devastation from their selfishness, but those who plant for the benefit of the Spirit will harvest eternal life from the Spirit." (Galatians 6:7-8)

This week wins the prize for worst week ever.
Well, so far.

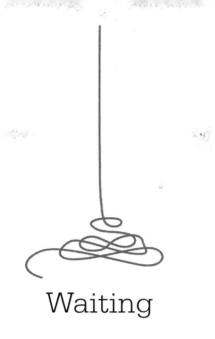

Waiting

I'm tired of fighting. I'm tired of crying. I'm tired of being sad. I'm tired of counseling. I'm tired of reading books on marriage. I'm tired of talking to people about my marriage. I'm even tired of *thinking* about my marriage.

I am not a woman who has slacked off in the working-on-my-marriage department. In a period of eighteen years, I read—if I had to guess—more than a hundred books on marriage or relationships or boundaries or holiness. I've been to nine counselors—some with, some without my then-husband. I attended a recovery group for my codependency and have worked through the twelve steps. I had two mentors. I am self-aware. I know my flaws. I have begged God to help me and heal me.

But I am weary. And, I'm realizing, there is not one magic tip that's going to revolutionize my relationship. Not that I don't have immeasurable room for improvement and not that I've learned all there is to learn about marriage, but I think it's safe to say, there's no one thing hidden somewhere that I have yet to stumble upon that will solve everything.

I know the basics. We should be kind to each other, we should respect each other, we should serve each other, we should take care of each other. But many years of muck and mire and hiddenness is making those things near impossible, and right now, there is not one thing else I believe I can do.

So I am praying. I am attempting to hold my tongue. And I am waiting.

I heard author Henry Cloud say that *transformation is truth plus grace plus time.* If that's the case, all truth has been said to both of us; we both gave grace over those many years in not walking out prematurely, and we've given grace in the choice to separate (even if it doesn't look like grace to the outside world). And now, all that's left is time.

I have a dear friend who has wanted to add to her family through adoption for more than five years. She has prayed and waited and prayed some more. The door seemed to close. Then another door seemed to open: fostering. She currently has the most beautiful child living in her home, living with her family every day. But the waiting continues. They have recently been told that long-term guardianship is a possibility. Wait some more. So she bathes and feeds and loves and waits and prays and her heart grows more and more attached, and I am watching her be transformed as she learns to hold loosely. She has no choice but to hold loosely and to wait. Her heart aches for this sweet child. In this moment, she has no idea if she will raise this child into adulthood or if she will be letting go before another birthday rolls around.

I cannot stand waiting. I hate living in limbo. But I have to admit that there is a beauty that only comes in the waiting. And really, what's the hurry? All we've got is time. But the time that we're after isn't the kind that just ticks away aimlessly. We need to be desperate to see God show up. Is he going to heal? What will that look like? What's he after in all this? Can he change my heart to want what he wants? Can there be a true brokenness that leads to a true repentance in our situation? Could there be more than one kind of miracle here? I don't know.

And yet, God is the one who is testing and refining us. Our so-called human enemies are not capable of that. There is not a person or persons for us to really blame for our on-hold circumstances. A court or a bank or a church or a man cannot keep us from where God wants us. So if we're not *there* yet—whatever *there* might look like—it's because God wants us *here*.

I can wait as long as I know God is waiting with me. I can stand on solid ground because the ground is God and not my somewhat ridiculous circumstances. People can think what they want and be angry with me and kick me while I'm down till next Sunday, but my God is my Father and my Husband and he is not disappointed in me or angry with me. He knows my heart, he knows I'm desperately trying to do what's right, he pursues me, he cares about my life and my sadnesses. He doesn't make me beg, and, yes, he loves me. Some days it feels as if he's the only one, which I know isn't true.

But even if that were the case, even if God were the only one who loved us, his love is enough. His love will always so completely be enough. We might be messes right now. But he can and will make something beautiful with us and out of our lives. We may have to wait and wait and wait, but he *will* come through. And all of it will be all right.

A Prayer

Spirit, I am so impatient. How I wish transformation could happen overnight. I want this trial of mine to be over . . . I'm so done with it. But you aren't. If it's still going on, it's because you must have something for me in this. Walk with me, please, and reveal your love to me, even in the waiting season, even in the unraveling. Amen.

A Next Good Step

There is a season for everything. There is a season to just sit there when you don't know what else to do. And there is a season to get up and do something—anything—when you've been sitting too long. Figure out what your balance is between being and doing, and don't go overboard with either during this difficult time.

A Way Forward

GOD proves to be good to the [woman] who
passionately waits,
    to the woman who diligently seeks.
It's a good thing to quietly hope,
    quietly hope for help from God.
(Lamentations 3:25 *THE MESSAGE*)

You already see what is about to happen today.

Happiness

My children and I have been looking at homes for a little while now. It is time to take that next step, and I just found out that my offer on the house my kids and I want was accepted. But, here's the thing. I wasn't expecting to get the house. I don't mean that my offer wasn't competitive enough. I'm talking about the God part of the equation.

Don't get me wrong. . . . I believed Jesus had told me that he was preparing a place that the three of us would love. I honestly felt him tell me that. Or, at least, I *wanted to believe* that I felt him tell me that.

I believed that God would provide for us, because I really feel that he has done that in a lot of huge ways over many years. Ahh, except that perhaps I haven't really, deep down, believed that he has come through, is coming through, and therefore would be coming through for me specifically any-time soon.

I sat on a dear friend's couch last night, celebrating the news about the house, and I said, through happy tears, "I just needed this so much. I haven't had really good news in such a long time." And she said, "Yeah, like since Jack's birth!" (My son is now a teenager.) She was kidding, of course, but then again, that's almost how it has felt lately, and apparently how it's even looking to my friends. (You know you're in a par-ticularly low spot when your friends find themselves praying things like, "Just throw her a bone, please, Jesus!")

I love God with my whole heart. But I think he and I have some work to do in this area, because I have seen mighty and gorgeous things happen to people I love, whereas for years I've seen only sweet and small God-things happen to me to keep me going. When you pray for something for years and years—and I mean, really pray, for something you think God would want for you—and it doesn't come to pass, you start to feel looked over. Forgotten, maybe, or intentionally left out. Abandoned. Unloved.

God promises that "no good thing does he withhold" (Psalm 84:11 NIV). But my life does not (from my small, skewed point of view) attest to that every day. Many good things have I felt him withhold from me. And a few really important things—that I thought he would've wanted for me, sincerely—like adopting a child internationally or a healed and whole marriage.

So, I've been begging him for this house and asking friends to pray for this house and hoping beyond hope, at least for my kids' sake, that he would come through. I have been praying, *Please, please, please, I'm begging you. I know you can but I don't know if you will. But please.* And yet I did not expect him to come through for me, although I knew we wouldn't be homeless. I knew, somehow, we would have a place to live.

I just didn't expect it to be the most lovely home I've ever lived in. A view of gorgeous, tall trees, with a trail for biking, a basketball court my son could walk to, and a neighborhood swimming pool. A home that my kids would love instantly. Yes, I knew God would take care of us, but I'm sad to say that I thought it would be the bare minimum. I didn't really believe that he would provide actual happiness.

But then my realtor called and told me we got the house. And as I stood in Target and cried, I recognized that the tears I was crying were tears of relief, of joy, of being taken care of, of being *happy.*

My hope is in Christ, not in my circumstances. I know that. I know what it feels like to be bottomed out, to have nothing to look forward to but being with Jesus.

But for today . . . today I have woken up with heavenly hope *and* some earthly hope tossed in.

A Prayer

Father, I am happy today! It's been a while. And I know my mood can change with the wind. But for this moment, I am gloriously happy and I thank you for that. Please help me enjoy it! Amen.

A Next Good Step

When was the last time you felt happy? Like, actually, circumstantially happy? When everything in your present moment felt really good and you just couldn't complain about anything? If it has been a while, then it's time for you to do something fun, something that makes you smile. Make a list of your top ten favorite things to do, and then do one of them in the next few days.

A Way Forward

"The people whose God is the Lord are truly happy!" (Psalm 144:15)

I face my birthday looking back on a year that kicked my ass. I am desperate for a fresh start physically, emotionally, spiritually, and relationally.

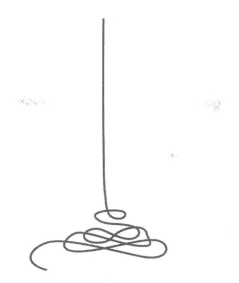

Expectations

During my separation, I celebrated my seventeenth and eighteenth wedding anniversaries. Well, I'm divorcing and alone these days, so I suppose *celebrating* isn't the right word. Observing, maybe. Reflecting, for sure.

All those years ago, I stood in front of a group of people I loved and stood before a man that I was crazy about, and I told God that I would take that man to have and to hold from that day forward, for better and for worse, for richer and for poorer, in sickness and in health, to love and to cherish, till death us do part.

I expected that I would be able to do those things. I'm sure I was daunted and thought it would be difficult. I knew that I might mess up from time to time, and that being an adult child of divorce wouldn't help, but I did not think we would have so much conflict. And I never would have predicted that *love* and *cherish* were concepts that would cause us both pain because of how aware we were of their absence. I never guessed that I would get to a place of such heartache that I would consider walking away prior to the death that was supposed to part us; or worse, that I would actually pray for my death to end the marital misery. No, I didn't see any of that coming as I stood there in my glimmering white dress in that sacred space surrounded by people who loved me, with God as my witness.

Expectations are a slippery slope. Some people expect much too much, of themselves, of others, of their circumstances, and they get disappointed constantly. Others expect little and walk around with a chip on their shoulders. I'm somewhere in the middle, or so it seems.

I ran across a list of my marriage expectations that a counselor had suggested I write:

I expected we would argue a lot, but . . .

I expected him to like me.

I expected him to love me.

I expected him to love Jesus passionately.

I expected we would do ministry together.

I expected him to be my best friend.

I expected him to always tell me the truth.

I expected us to make decisions together.

I expected he'd always make me laugh.

I expected him to treat me like an equal, adult partner.

And to that list, I added this last one just recently, in a quiet and sad moment.

I expected I wouldn't cry as much as I have.

All of the things I listed above had to do with someone else. All of them were contingent upon something someone else would say or do. But that wasn't fair. What was I expecting of myself? I am learning, in my divorce, that my energy is better spent thinking about what kind of person I want to be and how I can place my hope in God and not others. I've got enough to work on in myself to keep me occupied for the rest of my life; I need to keep my focus on who God wants me to be and not on someone else's journey.

A Prayer

God, you are the only one I can expect the world from. Help me expect from others only to be human. Help me expect myself to stumble, fall, and get back up again. But from you, I gratefully expect you to love me no matter what and to wipe away my tears when my heart breaks. Thank you. Amen.

A Next Good Step

Begin a list of things that you can realistically expect from yourself, such as, *I will take care of my health, I will take care of my children, I will read one book each month.* And start a list of things you can expect from God, such as, *he will never leave me, he will walk through the fire and deep waters with me, he will love me no matter what.* The more you focus on what you are responsible for and how God will be there for you, the more your expectations of others will slowly fade.

A Way Forward

Lord, in the morning you hear my voice.

In the morning I lay it all out before you.

Then I wait expectantly. (Psalm 5:3)

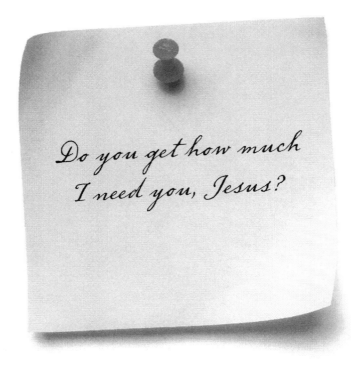

Good-byes

I have lists all over my desk right now. This week's to-dos. Insurance choices. Handyman priorities. A what-I'm-taking-with-me list and a what-goes-into-what-room-once-we-get-there list. Because my kids and I are moving. It's almost here. A couple of months ago we found our next home, and then we sat and waited for it to come to pass. And soon it will.

So now I have paint to buy, furniture to order, utilities to remove my name from, utilities to turn on, mail to have forwarded, things to clean, things to pack, things to throw away.

I'm overwhelmed. I'm reminding myself that in a couple months, I should be settled into my new place and all will be well, figuratively speaking.

But the other morning, as I walked up to my front door, leaves crunching under my feet, I felt Jesus say, "It's time to start saying good-bye." *I know*, I said, immediately longing to have a few extra minutes to sit on my favorite bench that overlooks our pond. But before my thoughts could get too far down the road on how much I'm going to miss this home, this sweet place, this land and my pond, Jesus continued, "And I don't just mean the house."

Oh.

Right.

Because other than signing the actual divorce papers, moving is just about as officially *over* as it can get. There will be no more limbo. There will be no more old-life-minus-one-person. This will be a complete leaving behind, a moving forward, a starting over, an entirely new life. It's time to really say my good-byes.

But how do you say good-bye to a home? To the place that sheltered your soul? That you thought would be where you lived out the rest of your days? And, in the exact same moment, how do you say good-bye to a husband? To the man you loved and had children with? To the man who has hurt you? To the man you have hurt? To the man who was your husband but soon will no longer be?

I sat on my couch—the couch that has held hundreds of conversations with Jesus, the couch that I am not taking with me but wish I were, the couch I'm leaving behind so my kids will still feel at home when they come back here for week-ends—and I glanced at the artwork on the wall, given to me by a friend. It has mocked me this past year, and I'm surprised I didn't take it down months ago. It's the "love is . . ." passage from 1 Corinthians 13. My eye stopped on *love never fails*.

But my love did fail, I said through tears. *I was selfish. I was critical. I wasn't strong enough to look for help earlier and insist upon it until we got it. I was too much to bear. My love failed. And now,* more tears, *I am getting a divorce.* (That was the first time I actually said that phrase out loud. . . . I've said *we're divorcing* and *my husband is divorcing me* and *I'm attending DivorceCare*, but I've never said out loud, until today, that *I am getting a divorce.*)

I don't know how to say good-bye to all of this at once. I don't know how to walk away. I do not still love my husband, but I'm not a monster. We have been in each other's lives for twenty-five years. We have two children. Although a lot of our relationship was very hard and extremely sad, not every moment of it was. I do still care. I want him to heal and live a good life.

So, in a simple, quiet act of farewell, because I did not know what else to do, I placed two sheets of paper on my kitchen counter. One said at the top, "God has done great things for me (here), and I am filled with joy." The other said, "I thank my God every time I remember you." I spent a couple of days fill-ing those sheets of paper with sweet memories and parting gratitudes for the home that has sheltered me for more than four years and for the man who was my husband for almost two decades.

I will thank God over these lists. I will cry. I will let Jesus walk me through this grieving process as I pack and reminisce, as I watch things die and be buried and change. And then I will wait for the new life to come, for the new thing he wants to do in me that I cannot yet see or feel or believe.

A Prayer

Heavenly Father, there are so many things to say good-bye to . . . not just to my house or to my husband but to who I was, to the life I've been living. Please help me through this process. Help me look back in gratitude, help me let go, help me accept my reality, and help me move on. Amen.

A Next Good Step

Our hearts are in a vulnerable place. The decisions we make with our thoughts now will help shape us as we move on. Even if you think you'll have nothing to be thankful for, I want you to begin a gratitude list for your marriage. Sit with the list and tell God what you'll miss about it.

A Way Forward

There's a season for everything
        and a time for every matter under the heavens:
        a time for giving birth and a time for dying,

a time for planting and a time for uprooting
   what was planted,
a time for killing and a time for healing,
a time for tearing down and a time for
   building up,
a time for crying and a time for laughing,
a time for mourning and a time for dancing,
a time for throwing stones and a time for
   gathering stones,
a time for embracing and a time for avoiding
   embraces,
a time for searching and a time for losing,
a time for keeping and a time for throwing away,
a time for tearing and a time for repairing,
a time for keeping silent and a time for speaking,
a time for loving and a time for hating,
a time for war and a time for peace.

                  (Ecclesiastes 3:1-8)

I'm walking through the grief, and
I'm inviting it to sit beside me
and teach me.
I refuse to just skim over it,
even if it hurts.
And it does.

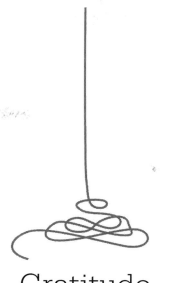

Gratitude

Several years ago during a struggle in my professional life, I learned a hugely transformational lesson about gratitude in the midst of trials. I discovered the importance of thanking God *now* and looking for God *now*, in the middle of the trouble.

And, you see, this thing we're now in—this separation or divorce—is a bona fide crisis. I have had innumerable hard times swing through my life over the years—just as you have, I'm certain. I have read pretty much every book on getting through a trial, and I have about a zillion big and little tips on how to navigate the dark and difficult waters of this life. But nothing, and I mean nothing, has worked for my heart like this ridiculously basic practice of reciting all that's good in my life.

Yet, this divorce crisis is bringing much subtler graces, and I'm having to squint to see them. Some days it feels that I'm just becoming a smaller person, that I'm shrinking, that I've lost portions of myself. But I'm choosing to look for the good that comes, and here is what I'm seeing:

I love my kids more and better. We talk more. I'm more protective of them, in a good way. I'm being more consistent with them. I'm teaching them things that wouldn't have crossed my mind to teach them if not for our current situation.

There is a peace in our home now that I haven't experienced in years, that my kids haven't experienced in their entire lives. The price a family pays when the home front is chaotic is difficult to measure, but I know it's costly and fracturing.

My thoughts are not consumed, as they once were. Yes, I still think about how my kids are dealing with all this, and what new antic has just played out, and how this divorce is affecting me now and will affect me down the road. But if you could have seen inside my hurting, confused mind before life took its current turn, you would not have believed how much mental energy I expended simply trying get through another day.

My friends mean even more to me now, which I didn't think was possible.

My sadness makes me slower and less ambitious, so I'm trying to see and enjoy the smaller things around me . . . the leaves, holding a friend's baby, letting little girls put barrettes in my hair while their mommy takes a much-needed nap, tea with a friend who understands what I'm going through.

I'm grateful. I'm not just grateful for whatever redemption may come down the line, but I'm grateful for today. For the quiet. For the peace of mind. For the relief. For the knowing I did all I could. For the support and those standing alongside me. For the beginnings of trying to understand that somehow I am in the will of God. I'm even grateful for those who call me out and are being unkind, because I'm clinging more tightly to Jesus because of them. Lately, if I look really hard, I see lots of small, good things.

As I started my morning walk today, I almost immediately said out loud, "The LORD has done great things for [me] and [I] am filled with joy" (Psalm 126:3 NIV). And then I purposed to spend the entirety of my walk focusing on gratitude.

I started by listing off one area: my health. I thought of all the ways that I have been crazy blessed. I can walk, I can run, I can see clearly, I can breathe in deeply, I can eat almost any food I want, I can hear the birds, I have not had one signifi-cant health problem in all my forty-plus years. Amazing when you think about it, truly amazing. And then I said, continuing out loud as I walked, "Thank you. The LORD has done great things for me and I am filled with joy."

I repeated this practice through lists of my children and my friends and God's word and the ways he has wired me up and the opportunities I've been given. When I was finished, I started in on my trials. I won't go into that crazy list right here, but it was long and it was sobering, saying all my life's hardships out loud at one time like that. But then I reminded myself that I have seen beauty come from ashes in each one of those things . . . the things that were done to me and the things that I did to myself. I thanked God for them and I said again, "The Lord has done great things for me . . . even these things . . . and I am filled with joy."

And then I thought about my "right now." I thought about my current sadness and I said out loud, "I'm really sad right now. But you are with me. And I'm angry right now. But you are with me. And I feel like I'm messing up. But you are with me. And no matter what comes along, you will be with me and you will never leave me and your word promises that I have a hope and that I can do anything through you and that, best of all, you love me. You will always love me."

Now, this is where I am supposed to tell you that I felt lighter as I got in my car and drove home, that I felt changed somehow. I did not. I sometimes do after moments like this, but today I did not. However, for the length of my walk, I had set down my burdens to free myself to be grateful. And then I asked God to remind me throughout just this day of the things I listed. So I expect a grateful, quiet spirit to follow me over the next few hours. And sometimes that's enough. Sometimes that needs to be enough.

A Prayer

"Accept, O Lord, our thanks and praise for all that you have done for us. We thank you for the splendor of the whole creation, for the beauty of this world, for the wonder of life, and for the mystery of love. We thank you for the blessing of family and friends, and for the loving care which surrounds us on every side. We thank you for setting us at tasks which demand our best efforts, and for leading us to accomplishments which satisfy and delight us. We thank you also for those disappointments and failures that lead us to acknowledge our dependence on you alone." —*Book of Common Prayer*

A Next Good Step

Today if you find yourself between a rock and a hard place of any kind, I want to encourage you to search after gratitude, because one thing I know is this: deep joy always, always follows deep gratitude. Place a blank piece of paper on your kitchen counter or on your desk at work next to your computer, write "great things God has done" at the top of the sheet; and each time you pass that paper today or glance at it as you reach for the phone, write down just one great thing in your life. It can be anything from *I didn't run out of coffee this morning* to *I'm grateful for a day without tears*. Then take that piece of paper on a walk this evening or to bed with you tonight and put two and two together that all good gifts come from the Father. And then thank him for those gifts, and wait for the joy to start filling in the dry cracks and empty spaces. Because it will, if you let it.

A Way Forward

"The word of Christ must live in you richly. Teach and warn each other with all wisdom by singing psalms, hymns, and spiritual songs. Sing to God with gratitude in your hearts." (Colossians 3:16)

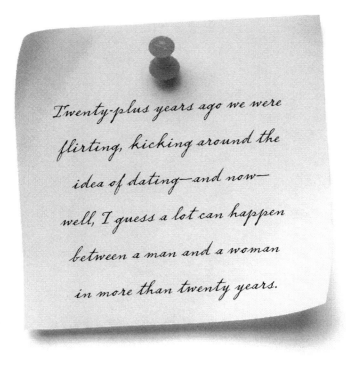

Twenty-plus years ago we were flirting, kicking around the idea of dating—and now— well, I guess a lot can happen between a man and a woman in more than twenty years.

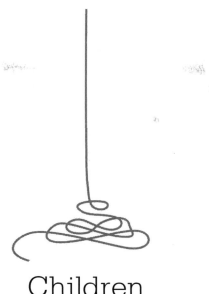

Children

W e're officially in that groove of my kids splitting their weekends between homes. I wasn't prepared for this. Kids aren't supposed to divvy up their time between parents. And parents aren't supposed to give up their kids for a certain amount of time each week. But we're beyond *supposed to* right now.

I have unwittingly replicated my childhood in my children's lives and that is perhaps my largest regret as a person, as a Christian, and as a mother. Early in this marriage, children were brought into the mix and I hoped, crossing my spiritual fingers, that it would somehow turn out better, if for no other reason than because we had Jesus, and surely he wouldn't let us flail—or fail—indefinitely.

I have a daughter and a son, both teenagers. I love them both like crazy. So it kills me to admit that they have grown up under the covering of a difficult Christian marriage that was as full of conflict as it was of prayer. Talk about some mixed messages. (Talk about *therapy*.)

I could write a book on how I've unintentionally passed along my dysfunctional tendencies to my children, with charts and graphs of my predictions and concerns. But that will do no one any good. So I will offer a few pieces of guidance as you walk your children through this experience of separation and divorce.

Find them someone they will feel comfortable talking with, someone other than you or your ex. It could be a trusted teacher, youth pastor, aunt or uncle, friend of the family, or a counselor. Anyone who knows your situation and shares your values will do. Then do whatever you can to get them to spend time together. Don't worry that you don't know what's being talked about, don't worry if they are complaining about you (they probably are). Just get them talking.

Plan fun things with them. My kids and I now go out for dinner every Wednesday before youth group, and we try to do an at-home movie night every few weeks. Your life may be falling apart, but help theirs stay as fun and light as possible. They are still children. Their childhoods are being cut short because of your circumstances, so infuse joy into your family as creatively as you can.

Do not talk to your children about your spouse, unless in a positive light. I am not saying to keep your children completely in the dark, especially if they're older. Some things they do need to know. But do not place them in the middle of you two in any way. Do not use your children to relay messages to your spouse; if you do, your kids will remember being go-betweens and will resent the weight this places on them. Encourage them to communicate with their parent and to spend time with him or her when their schedules allow.

Cut them slack, but not too much. Their lives have turned upside down, so a mental health day off from school won't kill them, nor will your helping them with their chores every once in a while. On the other hand, they need structure now more than ever so you're going to have to be the good cop *and* the bad cop, even when it's hard and even when you're tired. Be their parent, not their friend. Friendship will come down the line.

Your children will look back on your separation and divorce as a defining moment in their lives, no matter the outcome. The best thing you can do for them is to be appropriately authentic with them, letting them see that you are finding your strength in God. And that, in and of itself, will give them strength.

"Children are resilient." I have heard this a thousand times. I have *said* this a thousand times. I no longer buy it. "Children are resilient" is said by people who don't want to face the reality that their actions affect the children in their lives. Here's what I'm coming to fully believe: God knew this was going to happen, and he has prepared me and my children for it. This is not God's "Plan B" for my life or for my children's lives. They are not doomed to limp through the rest of their lives emotionally and relationally deficient. They are not destined for bad marriages. This struggle can be used for good in their lives, if they'll let it. God *has been* taking care of them; God *is* taking care of them; and God *will* take care of them.

A Prayer

"God our Father, you see your children growing up in an unsteady and confusing world: Show them that your ways give more life than the ways of the world, and that following you is better than chasing after selfish goals. Help them to take failure, not as a measure of their worth, but as a chance for a new start. Give them strength to hold their faith in you, and to keep alive their joy in your creation; through Jesus Christ our Lord. Amen." —*Book of Common Prayer*

A Next Good Step

Ask your children to name one thing they love to do but haven't done in a while and then get it on your calendar.

A Way Forward

All your children will be disciples of the Lord—
   I will make peace abound for your children.
(Isaiah 54:13)

Lord, you came through for me!

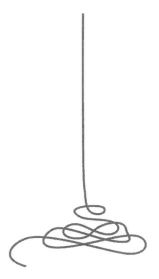

Loneliness

I settle into my favorite position in the bed, turning toward the center. I own a dual-side heating blanket, meaning each side can have its own setting. I reach my foot toward the other side of the bed, toward the line of demarcation. Cold sheets. Literally and figuratively. It sends a shock to my system almost every night. Cold sheets, lonely heart. I am lonely in this big, quiet bed of mine. Not for my specific marriage, but I am lonely for companionship, for a marriage. For the marriage I was created to have.

Not only do I feel the pangs of loneliness at nighttime but also when one of my kids says something totally funny. When I'm dragging the recycling bin to the end of the driveway on a winter's night. When I'm sitting in church, either with my kids or all alone if they're not with me for the weekend. There is a chasm deep and wide when I look around the sanctuary and see couples who are solid and steady all around me, and then there's just me, no *us* anymore.

I am a raging introvert. I am fiercely independent. I would choose time alone over time with a large group of people any day. I like doing things a certain way. I'm stubborn. Living alone has its advantages, I must admit.

But here's the thing. My marriage had been wobbly and precarious for so long that I grieved the loss of the partnership I had hoped for long before we separated. Still, there is a loneliness that accompanies me wherever I go, forever reminding me that I am now alone, really and truly *alone*. I knew this going in. When I was released to separate, I knew in the back of my head that I was trading fifty years to come of *married* and lonely for, possibly, fifty years of *single* and lonely. Both are rough in their own unique ways.

When do you feel the most alone, dear friend? Were there little moments that you used to revel in together as a couple, like reading the Sunday paper with coffee and breakfast in bed, or pizza night on Fridays—things like that? Maybe even just having a "wingman" at extended family gatherings or someone to pick up the milk that you forgot?

This lonely season has offered up several lessons to me. It turns out that I am more capable of being good company for myself than I thought I would be. I've learned to eat at restaurants alone, and—gasp—go to the movies all by myself. I can hang out at the library or a coffee shop for hours at a time. I've even taken the train to neighboring towns, just to explore them at my own pace.

I'm also being reminded that my friends are even more amazing than I originally thought. They check in on me with e-mails, texts, phone calls, notes, dinner invitations, and tea dates. I'm so loved and surrounded and held up. Loneliness can draw you tighter inside or it can propel you to find comfort in others. Just make sure that you choose your company wisely during this time.

And this, the best re-learning of all: God is so completely with me, every single moment of my living and breathing and walking and sighing and waiting. Scripture promises that God is especially close to the brokenhearted (Psalm 34:18), and I believe that our current circumstances qualify us for those extraordinary measures of intimacy. He is always present with us, but during a hard time, I picture him bending down even lower to minister, heal, and bless.

Discover yourself, seek out dear friends, and lean into the Lord.

By the way, tonight, I think I might turn on both sides of my heating blanket and scooch over to the center.

A Prayer

"Almighty God, whose Son had nowhere to lay his head: Grant that those who live alone may not be lonely in their solitude, but that, following in his steps, they may find fulfillment in loving you and their neighbors; through Jesus Christ our Lord. Amen." —*Book of Common Prayer*

A Next Good Step

This week, plan one activity to do alone that you've never done alone. Set up a coffee date with a close friend, and spend some extra time with God.

A Way Forward

I am the LORD your God,

who grasps your strong hand,

who says to you,

"Don't fear; I will help you."

(Isaiah 41:13)

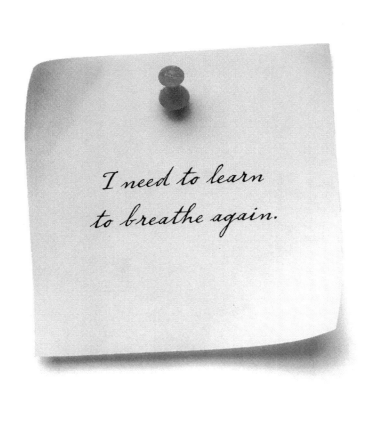

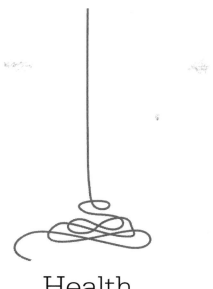

Health

I have lived enough of life to now know that I cannot control one iota of my circumstances. So when a dark season descends upon my life, I try to do everything that I can to be as physically, emotionally, and spiritually healthy as possible. Hard times pull more out of me, and I need my reserves to be full to overflowing as they tend to get depleted more rapidly when I'm carrying a heavy burden.

Several years ago, one such season cropped up—the professional struggle I previously mentioned—and at that time in my life, I had not been exercising, nor did I eat well. I would even go through a box of Milk Duds a day, always ridiculously wondering in the back of my head why I felt sluggish. But when the work struggle barreled into my life all those years ago, I sat up a bit taller and evaluated what I was and wasn't doing with my body. The day that the bad news walked through my door, I literally put on my gym shoes (yes, I can refer to them as gym shoes because they were my actual pair from high school from twenty years earlier; goes to show how little I'd used them), and I ran down the block. Although I knew I was attempting to run from my problem, I found it interesting that running was my knee-jerk reaction. So I laced up those old shoes the next day, and the next, and the next, and started a habit of running. I also took up yoga at the suggestion of a dear friend. I found both of these activities to be empowering, as I never considered myself to be an athlete of any kind. I changed my eating habits just a tad. Although I still ate candy, I added two items to my daily menu: I began to drink green tea at my quiet time each morning and some chamomile tea, when possible, in the afternoon or evening. I began drinking at least one, if not two, fruit and veggie smoothies each day as well. Last, I made sure I was getting as much sleep as I could. All these years later, most of these changes still play a part in my life, and I know I have more energy and am healthier because of it.

Emotionally, I amped things up a bit by committing to daily journaling to process the thoughts and feelings that I was flooded with and overwhelmed by. I also got back in touch with a counselor I had been seeing a couple of years earlier and scheduled biweekly appointments. And I made sure that I was spending time with my girlfriends, who loved me and wanted to support me.

And spiritually, I made sure to begin each day in God's presence. I knew I couldn't get through the trials that lay ahead without his power, his help, his guidance, and his peace. I clung to him, I brought my fears to him, and I begged him for help and comfort. I ran to God and let him walk me through that season.

So much of life is out of our control. Some days, we can feel too busy to take care of ourselves, and yet, it's always our choice. Even on the most hectic day, a twenty-minute walk or journaling session is possible. God created us with a body, mind, and soul. We are to take care of and nourish these gifts. And when we do, we will be able to handle the *uncontrollables* of life with a bit more grace.

A Prayer

"Creator of the universe, fount of things strange and wonderful, praise to you for the mystery of my being. Help me put myself together." —Kathleen Fischer and Thomas Hart

A Next Good Step

Every day is a clean slate. Today, why don't you consider making one small change that will help you improve your health? Take a brisk walk, sign up for a Bible study or yoga class, or even make yourself a smoothie and sneak some veggies into your diet.

A Way Forward

"Or don't you know that your body is a temple of the Holy Spirit who is in you? Don't you know that you have the Holy Spirit from God, and you don't belong to yourselves?" (1 Corinthians 6:19)

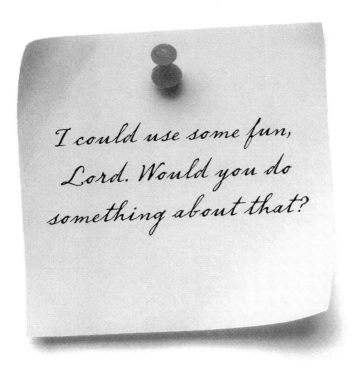

I could use some fun, Lord. Would you do something about that?

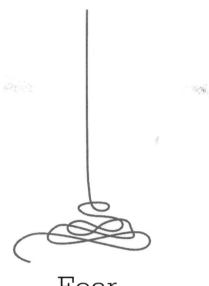

Fear

My first Thanksgiving without my kids: I gave them to my husband for the day, and I cried as I drove away. And now Christmas is here.

I'm reading the first two chapters of the Gospel of Luke this month as I choose to reflect on the Christmas story and its implications for my life these days. And I found something that surprised me. In the 132 verses of those two chapters, an angel tells three different main characters not to be afraid.

He tells Zechariah not to fear, because his prayer has been heard.

He tells Mary not to fear, because God has a surprise for her (quite the understatement, don't you think?).

And he tells the shepherds not to fear, because he's here to announce a great and joyful event.

I think I underestimate the part that fear plays in my life. I've wrongly considered myself to not be a fearful person; in essence, I really do fear quite a bit. What might happen tomorrow? What might not happen tomorrow? A sadness may lurk just under the surface of every experience for the rest of my life. I could make hugely wrong decisions. I could profoundly mess up my kids. I could miss God's purpose for me. You know, little fears like that.

But what I'm seeing in Scripture today—as I look at Luke's account of the arrival of Jesus—is the common theme of *not* fearing, of being told to not be afraid, as if that's something we can choose to do (because it must be).

My head knows every single thing there is to know about worry and fear:

It doesn't add even an hour to my life.

It isn't a proactive barrier that will make potential bad news easier to bear.

It takes my mind off the present.

It's basically saying I don't believe that there is a loving God guiding my life.

I know all of these things about worry and fear. And, for the most part, the truth of God's love does make its way to my heart and reside there.

There is a reason, I'm sure, that Jesus says *do not be afraid* about a zillion times. It's because, in part, he knows our tendency to jump to fear as our default reaction. But I think it's also because he knows something that we keep failing to truly integrate into our lives. That his Father, who is also our Father, really loves us. That our Father is not out to get us. That he's not coming up with wild schemes to mess with our heads and leave us feeling untended. That anything that comes our way—and I really mean *anything*—has been lovingly sifted through his hand before it enters our lives.

Author Ann Voskamp says in her book *One Thousand Gifts* that "all fear is but the notion that God's love ends." My life is proclaiming with each catch of my breath from worry that deep down I fear God's love for me can come to a stop. If only, in those slivers of moments between a worry emerging and my entire body responding to that worry, I could remind myself that God is love (1 John 4:8). This means he cannot stop being something that he fundamentally is, nor can he stop acting out of his character.

So today, this is how I'm choosing to prepare my heart for Christ. I will lay down my fears for this day. I will set aside my dread and place it in my Father's capable hands. I will ask Jesus to help me be courageous, resting my weary mind in the hopes that space will be cleared for sweeter, truer thoughts to fill my soul.

A Prayer

"Let nothing disturb you. Let nothing frighten you. All things pass away: God never changes. Patience obtains all things. Those who have God find they lack nothing; God alone suffices." —St. Teresa of Avila (1515–82)

A Next Good Step

What are you afraid of? Make a list. Imagine yourself handing each fear over to God, and then walking away, knowing he's got it all under control.

A Way Forward

"You have nothing to fear. God has a surprise for you." (Luke 1:30 *THE MESSAGE*)

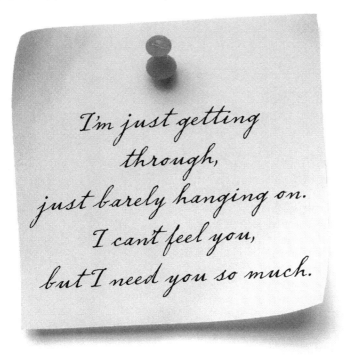

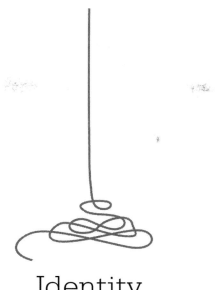

Identity

F rom my journal:

> Who am I, Lord? I have identified myself for so very long as
> unloved, incompetent . . . a woman who has had to work
> really hard to show people that she could make something
> of herself, that she is fit to be a mother and she is working
> on her marriage even though the marriage keeps failing. I
> hear the taunting: "You've done all this for yourself . . . these
> support groups and counseling . . . but your marriage is still
> the same. Doesn't that tell you something?"

Right now, I am a divorced woman. A single mother of two teenagers. A sad and lonely hot mess, minus the *hot*. I hope that this isolating, emptying time is just a bridge to who I will become. Right now, I have so little to give, and I can't picture my future with any clarity.

I don't want to be those labels anymore. There has got to be something else, someone better for me to be.

> But Jesus, my kids and my friends need me to be more than this, even on this bridge of in-between. Define me, Lord. Reinvent me. I'm stripped bare. Create new life here, where only old bones lie. Redeem this mess. Restore my soul. Make me new. Soften and strengthen this hard, scared heart of mine. My future is yours; it's all in your hands. To be honest, I fear greatly what you may ask of me. So please, please help me focus on how much you love me and how near you are to me. I love you and need you so much.

For fifteen years, I subconsciously pursued a super-busy, get-me-out-of-this-house, get-me-out-of-my-head over-achiever's life. The list of my achievements during those years is long, and I say that with humility because I believe deep down that God allowed those gifts to buoy up my soul during my sad marriage.

But now that the marriage has been removed from my daily life, I feel like a piece of old furniture. I feel like a shell. I feel like I don't need all those trappings that I once used to distract myself.

I was a dichotomy. A mother, friend, author, speaker, women's ministry director, AIDS team leader, developing-world traveler, social justice advocate. And yet—just as true—an emotionally broken, codependent, constantly hurting, failure of a wife. All of it, all at the same time.

There is a moment, a grieving, where you realize you are not who you thought you were. Just this morning, while driving home along familiar roads after dropping off my kids at school, I said out loud, "Who am I now?" And I scrolled back over some scenes from my life when I was so belittled, when I apologized for things that weren't my fault, when I cowered emotionally so as not to rock the boat. How much of my life was wasted trying to be someone that I wasn't, someone that I was never meant to be?

So if I'm old furniture, and if perhaps, someone were to come along who thought I had value, what would he have to do to restore me?

For starters, he'd clean off the surface to prepare it for the process. This would be a gentle washing away of wounds. I am not any of the names I have been called. I am not incompetent, incapable. I am not an angry woman. I am not . . . well, I am not a lot of things I was given the impression that I was.

Then he'd have to strip away the old layers, in my case, the roles I played that didn't fit. I am not defined by who I am married to, or whether I am married at all. I am not defined by the good I do outside of my home. I am not defined by the number of tears I cry or the number of recovery meetings I feel I must attend to get through.

And then he'd start applying new layers—this time, layers of truth. The base coat is what is true for us all: we are made in the image of God. Christ took on our sin because we couldn't pay the price for ourselves. After entering into a relationship with Jesus, the Holy Spirit dwells within us and will never leave us. We are precious and honored in his sight. Things like that.

But then this someone would move into the fun part . . . the colors, the design, the details. What makes me unique, what my purpose is, what my calling is. Everything has been stripped away, and he and I are looking at each other, and I'm waiting to hear what's next.

Time passes by, and the new truths sink in. This is where I am right now, I believe. The grieving will continue, and then at some point it will be behind me; but the healing . . . that will go on and on as I take on what God says about me and move forward, coming back into the world. I'm convinced that our truest identities emerge from the point where our brokenness is covered over by God's great love. And that is where our best stories will flow from.

A Prayer

"Dear God, when I see myself as you see me, then I will understand that this frail, tender, fearful, aching, singing, half-empty, shining, shadowed person is a whole being made especially by you for your love." —Joy Cowley

A Next Good Step

Think of one—only one—trait that you have never really liked about yourself. Ask God if he wants to change it, or maybe if he simply wants you to look at it in a different light.

A Way Forward

"God, not your marital status, defines your life."

(1 Corinthians 7:17 *THE MESSAGE*)

I cant take much more of this, God.

Not today.

So, please place me in a cleft in a

rock with your hand as my covering.

Hatred

The conversation with a friend was interrupted, but hours later, I remembered her unanswered question: "Do you hate him?"

Define hate, is what I thought to myself.

Do I wish we could carry on a civilized conversation? Yes.

Do I wish I would never have to see him again? Honestly? Sometimes.

Do I want to scream at him? Yep, occasionally.

Do I wish I could look him in the eye again? Yes. I'm so sad that I can't.

Do I wish him harm? No.

Do I wish I had never met him? No; I have my kids because of him.

Do I wish him well? Yes, actually.

Do I feel compassion for him? In my better moments, yes (and I'm gratefully having more better moments these days).

So do I hate him? Absolutely not.

My church is doing a sermon series on generosity. I'm all for that. I like being generous. Some of my best life moments have been times when I've been able to give a gift that surprised a friend or stranger. But this is already taking a different turn for me. The Holy Spirit is messing with me. I'm not a fan of the Spirit doing this.

This chapter isn't going to be about money. And although I thought it would be about my time and how I tend to hoard it selfishly, I don't think it's going to be about that either.

I'm pretty sure God wants me to be generous with my ex-husband. No, not send him flowers or anything. Not hang out with him against his will (although that might be kind of funny in a totally awkward way).

God wants me, if I'm discerning correctly, to be generous with my words, with my actions, with my attitudes.

I think he wants me to forgive lavishly.

To let the smaller offenses drop to the ground instantly.

To stop the rabbit from going down the trail each time a snarky thought comes to my mind.

To offer things that I have no obligation to offer.

To start speaking truth, even in small pieces, as respectfully and steadily as I can.

To pray for him.

To ask God to bless him.

It's interesting. Part of me so doesn't want to do this. Part of me thinks that doing these kinds of things is more or less extra credit—and just the fact that I'm not, you know, egging my old house is pretty darn Jesus-y of me. And yet, part of me saw this coming. Part of me had already been choosing small acts of rebellion against my sinful nature. I have been using the phrase "the high road" for a couple of months now already, so I think I was primed for this. Plus—*hello*—Jesus always, always took the high road. So, I'm pretty sure I'm supposed to take it as well.

My expectations are low, or at the very least, realistic. I do not expect a turnaround in this relationship. I do not expect a plea for forgiveness or to be forgiven. What I expect, though, is that something will happen to my heart that would not happen if I clenched my fists and told the Spirit that I do not want to love my enemy, thank you very much. In fact, my heart is already changing, with compassion sneaking its way into the crevices, as only the Spirit can do. And I've only just gotten started.

A Prayer

Long enough, GOD—
> you've ignored me long enough.
I've looked at the back of your head
> long enough. Long enough

I've carried this ton of trouble,
>   lived with a stomach full of pain.
Long enough my arrogant enemies
>   have looked down their noses at me.

Take a good look at me, God, my God;
>   I want to look life in the eye,
so no enemy can get the best of me
>   or laugh when I fall on my face.

I've thrown myself headlong into your arms—
>   I'm celebrating your rescue.
I'm singing at the top of my lungs,
>   I'm so full of answered prayers.
(Psalm 13 *THE MESSAGE*)

A Next Good Step

This is going to be super hard, but I want to challenge you to do one kind thing for your ex. Yep. If you're just not at a place to be able to do something tangible, take a few moments to pray for him. No matter your shared past, he is a creation of the same God who created you.

A Way Forward

"When someone gives you a hard time, respond with the energies of prayer, for then you are working out of your true selves, your God-created selves." (Matthew 5:44 *THE MESSAGE*)

I dont know where my children
are this weekend.
Trying to be grateful, though,
that you know.

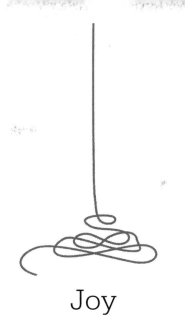

Joy

I am a melancholy personality. I love rainy days. I love staying in my pajamas for as long as possible. I love sleeping
in. As you've probably gathered by now, I love naps. I love
curling up on the couch with some tea and a good book. I love
lighting candles as the day starts turning to dusk.

I honestly love the hard times as much as the good times
because I learn so much more about myself and about Jesus
in the darkness than in the wide, open, light spaces. So, when
the clouds roll in, I assume my position of a frown and a

whimper, with my journal poised in my hand to record every moment of my newest sad tale.

Which is why it is so very important for me to look for joy. I commission myself to search it out in the grand moments, to look for it in the typical sweetness, and to chase it in the day-to-day. I make myself linger and laugh longer. I implore the Spirit to point out those fleeting flashes of time when I normally would miss the light.

One of those surprises snuck up on me one regular night, pre-separation, when I was driving my kids home from youth group. The sun was beginning to set and the sky was exploding with color. All I can say is that I felt compelled in that moment. I turned down a country road and pulled the car over next to a cornfield at nine o'clock at night, on a school night, and told the kids to get out. We stood by the side of the road and just watched the sky and sun change. And then my daughter starting singing a praise song to Jesus, telling him how much we all loved him, and in that instant my heart burst open. Tears came and I tried to take a mental snapshot of that moment. I closed my eyes and breathed in deeply, and I thanked Jesus for his love and beauty. And then we got back in the car and went home, changed.

We were quieter on the way home. And although it all cast a gentle shadow on us for maybe five minutes, something had shifted in me.

You see, life was hard for us right then and there. And we all weren't fans of what we were going home to. And I'm not typically known to be the kind of mom who pulls her car over to look at a sunset. But we needed joy. We needed to remember that God is bigger and life is not just about us and that there is beauty all around us at all times and we can be thankful even when things are awful.

So look for joy. Search it out. Beg Jesus for it. Keep your eyes wide open and your heart open too, just a bit. Let joy fill you up when the tears won't stop. Let it wash over you when you're feeling all alone. Let it crash through the anger and calm down your fears. And you will be surprised time and time again how Jesus can bring some light into the middle of your dark. You'll be even more surprised how it helps you forget your dark for just a little while.

A Prayer

"O Great Spirit of Surprise, dazzle us with a day full of amazing embraces; capricious, uncalculated caring; great hearts; kind souls; and doers of good deeds." —Molly Fumia

A Next Good Step

Spend ten minutes writing out a list of things that make you smile. Then go look for one of them today!

A Way Forward

Weeping may stay all night,
        but by morning, joy! (Psalm 30:5)

I feel lost. I look old and tired and used up.

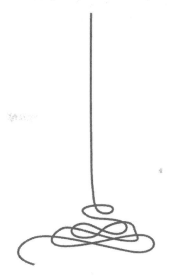

Friendship

I am not the woman that I thought I would be as a forty-something. And my circumstances are not the circumstances I thought I would be living through in my forties. I'm a bit more rough around the edges and a bit angrier than I would have predicted. But I'm also a lot more loved than I would have guessed too.

My closest friends know my darkness and have not left me to wade through it on my own. They also know my love for words, and for a recent birthday they gave me the indescribable gift of letters telling me what they love about me.

In these letters I was told that what they love about me most is that I am striving to be better, that I'm stronger than I think I am, that I have parts of me that just can't move on yet and that's OK. That I could mess everything up in my life, and they still won't walk away. That they see Jesus being formed in me. That they know I'm going to make it.

Not long ago, I found myself at a gathering of friends. The eight of us had weathered new babies, church campaigns, job changes, court dates, heart surgeries, and everything else that life can throw at you. Then one couple moved away. Several years passed, and a lot had changed.

The long-distance couple was back in town for the weekend, so I set up a reunion at my home. All these years later brought four more kids and one fewer husband. Seven adults and thirteen children—then-fourteen and under—crammed into my house for chaos and catching up. I'm a die-hard introvert, but this was heaven to me.

I was anxious before they came. We had always been eight. . . . Would it be awkward without my other half there? Would there be judgment? Would any of them push me a bit as to why I was still separated and not reconciled yet?

Turns out, I didn't give my friends enough credit. (Sorry, sweet ones.)

At one point, the seven of us adults were huddled in my living room, the kids dancing and running and playing all around. I was on the couch next to one of my girlfriends, and

I leaned my head on her shoulder and reached for her hand. I couldn't have felt more comfortable and sheltered than I did in that moment. "You can fall asleep if you want," she said to me. "No, I'm not tired; I'm just touch-deprived," I laughed. She patted me on the head, "Oh, sweetie," she said. Her husband was sitting across from us, on the floor, and said, "Let's all say something positive about Beth." Random and unexpected. I clapped with delight. "I love that idea!" I said needily, knowing full well these friendships provided a safe place for me to be my impoverished self.

Michelle: *You're cute.*

Casey: *The way you love words.*

Eric: *How much you value friendship.*

John: *You're a fighter, a butt-kicker.*

Parker: *You learn from your experiences and share with others what God teaches you.*

Erika: *The way you pursue our friendships.*

Casey: *You're a really good mother. You totally pour into your kids.*

Michelle: *You're generous.*

Erika: *You're brave.*

They had no idea what they did for me in those words, those friends who were about to go home as couples. They can't understand what I'm going through, although they are totally trying. They each gave me a long hug at the end of the night, even the guys. There was no judgment. There was just support. Just full words to fill the silences I've become used to. And more love than I could have asked for.

I'm surrounded by love. Jesus loves me, this I know. And Jesus knows me well enough to know that I need and crave human companionship. He knows that this separation has tapped into my biggest fears: how I fear being left behind, how I fear being rejected for who I am, how I fear not being liked just because I'm me. He knows that I love being alone but that a talk with a good friend can fill me up for days. He knew that I'd walk through the fire and deep waters in this life—most specifically in this past decade—and so he surrounded me with love in the form of others who, for some reason that I can't quite put my finger on, think I'm something special.

A Prayer

"You have blessed us, O God, with the gift of friendship, the bonding of persons in a circle of love. We thank you for such a blessing: for friends who love us, who share our sorrows, who laugh with us in celebration, who bear our pain, who need us as we need them, who weep as we weep, who hold us when words fail, and who give us the freedom to be ourselves. Bless our friends with health, wholeness, life, and love. Amen." —Vienna Cobb Anderson

A Next Good Step

Send a thank-you note to one of your closest friends today. If you find yourself friendless or isolated during this difficult season, ask God to bring someone into your life to walk beside you.

A Way Forward

"Two are better than one because they have a good return for their hard work. If either should fall, one can pick up the other. But how miserable are those who fall and don't have a companion to help them up!" (Ecclesiastes 4:9-10)

Forgiveness

You knew I'd have to touch on this eventually. Some of us may bristle at the prospect of having to forgive. Some of us have been hurt so deeply we can't even imagine forgiving the person who hurt us. But here's what I know. Whether the person who has hurt us has come to us and sincerely apologized or not, we are called to forgive. "If you forgive others their sins, your heavenly Father will also forgive you" (Matthew 6:14). Now, Jesus doesn't say that lightly. He doesn't say it like, *check your head and heart at the door*. I believe he says it knowing that it just might be one of the most difficult things you will ever have to do. The person who has hurt you may not deserve your forgiveness in your estimation. The person who has hurt you may still be hurting you. I completely understand.

I remember struggling with the issue of forgiveness a time or two in my life, and when I say a time or two, I mean thousands of times. I have been deeply hurt and wildly furious with people whom I have needed to forgive. I felt that forgiving them would be the equivalent of my saying what they had done was OK. And then it dawned on me that, basically, what I was doing when I chose to forgive them was letting them off *my* hook and putting them on *God's* hook. I was letting it go enough for God to do what he wanted and needed to in that situation. There was nothing I could do to retaliate, but I believe that God handles all justice in his timing and in his way. I've heard Beth Moore put it this way: get on your knees and tell on that person to Jesus, and God's arm of justice will swing right over you as you pray, and it will knock into the person in question. And we do not want to be in the way when God starts swinging.

Forgiveness is not a one-time event; it is a process. Now, it might be over quickly, such as when a friend hurts your feelings and she immediately apologizes, and you forgive her and move on. But in one particular drawn-out situation, I had to let someone off the hook (sometimes I imagined myself literally removing her from a hook) over and over again as thoughts of her would creep into my mind through a period of several years.

Another thing to keep in mind when deciding who you should forgive: you might think the offending party does not deserve forgiveness, but let me gently point out that neither do you and neither do I. I recently did an exercise in which I listed every wrongdoing of mine that I could muster up. You know what that list did for me? It knocked me off my little self-righteous soapbox. It opened my eyes to how much stuff I really have done that is horrific, how much I have done that is sin. How much stuff that Jesus had to die for, just because of me. I did not deserve his dying for me, his forgiveness, that great gift. And yet, he did it anyway. So, the next time you think that forgiveness is not due this person, take your own tally for a few moments and reconsider whether you'll offer forgiveness to them, as you would want someone else to do for you. Pastor Ray Pritchard says, "If you wait until you feel like forgiving, you're never going to forgive." It's a choice of your will, each and every time, but it will free you.

Keep in mind, though, that forgiving is not the equivalent of forgetting. Yes, I want to forget inasmuch as I don't want to walk around carrying resentments like pebbles in my pockets that seem to turn into boulders on their own. I want to forget in that I want to be able to look people in the eye who have hurt me and be able to keep my head up, be able to be genuinely kind to them. I want to forget and allow Christ to heal the wounds left by the trouble that has come into my life. I want to forget the details and not have to recall exact conversations from ten years ago, or even *one* year ago. I don't have the emotional energy or the room in my life to carry all of that with me anymore. I simply don't have room for all that old pain, and all this new hope and joy that I'm anticipating. But I don't want to forget altogether—and frankly, as humans, I'm not sure we ever really can—because it's important that we learn from our pain.

I would be remiss if I didn't add one more thought here. You and I are not blameless. We owe genuine apologies to someone, more than likely to our ex-spouses. Whether you feel like the bigger victim or whether you've yet to be apologized to, do your part and seek out forgiveness. We are all just human. You and I have done things that we can own and say we're sorry for and work on. I took an amends step with my then-husband several years ago, face-to-face, and then again through a letter as our divorce was becoming final. It will not be easy to own your part, apologize and try to learn from it; but this too will free you in ways you can't predict, and it will bring such honor to God.

A Prayer

"Lord, make us instruments of your peace. Where there is hatred, let us sow love; where there is injury, pardon; where there is discord, union; where there is doubt, faith; where there is despair, hope; where there is darkness, light; where there is sadness, joy. Grant that we may not so much seek to be consoled as to console; to be understood as to understand; to be loved as to love. For it is in giving that we receive; it is in pardoning that we are pardoned; and it is in dying that we are born to eternal life. Amen." —attributed to St. Francis of Assisi

A Next Good Step

Let me walk you through a situation where I realized I needed to forgive someone. Someone that I had known for a long time said something very hurtful to me. I was blindsided by this offense. And here's what I noticed: over the next several weeks, each time that offense popped into my mind, I would totally dwell on it. I wouldn't just think about it, as in, "Ouch, that really hurt"; oh no, I replayed the words of the e-mail, I made up amazing retorts that would put her in her place. But that wasn't healthy or a good use of my time. So, I sat down with my journal and I wrote out every detail that I could think of about this situation, including all the things I wished I had said in response. And then I wrote out a prayer, asking Jesus to forgive me for my horrible attitude toward her, and for all the time I had squandered thinking about it. I asked him to help me stop dwelling on it; I told him I forgave her and asked him to help me forgive her; I asked him to help me forget this incident; I ended my prayer with asking him to pour out a blessing over her life. And I completed the step by writing her a note of apology for my part in the incident. Then I closed the chapter. Try this process with someone in your life whom you need to forgive and see what happens in your heart.

A Way Forward

"Be tolerant with each other and, if someone has a complaint against anyone, forgive each other. As the Lord forgave you, so also forgive each other." (Colossians 3:13)

Hurts

I'm thinking about some of the men in my life and how they influenced my views of the world—but more importantly, of myself. Here are some of the harder messages I have received.

You are not worth committing to.

I don't love you enough to stay.

You have to tell me you love me even if you don't.

You are the reason you are treated the way you are.

You're fine for now; but, oh, wait. . . . She's prettier and better in almost every possible way.

I have no desire to get to know who you really are.

You don't deserve the respect to be told to your face that I've already moved on.

You make me uncomfortable, so I'm not going to enter in.

You are overdramatic and therefore shouldn't always be believed.

I will not be here for you no matter what.

You are your own worst enemy.

You need help.

You are an idiot.

You must beg for my affection.

As I foolishly dredged up all of this the other night, a couple of things came to mind. It was a sad and lonely kind of night, but then the Holy Spirit reminded me that not only had I learned harsh lessons from men, I had also learned innumerable good things about myself from my father and pastors and counselors and my guy friends and some old boyfriends—things like:

You are heard and understood.

You are protected.

You're a great leader, and I would follow you.

You are worth pursuing.

I'd trust you with my life.

You can't help but be beautiful.

You are funny and kind.

You are one of the most important people in my life.

You are worth standing up for.

You are an honorable woman.

I am on your side.

I love you.

I am grateful for all those words; they have healed me and painted over the harsher ones. And yet I know that there is only one who can speak the deepest, truest truths about me and into me. This is what God has to say:

You are precious and honored in my sight.

You will never be alone.

You are protected at all times.

You bring me joy.

I sing songs of delight over you.

I hear you and give you what you need.

I am transforming you into something beautiful.

I have adopted you as my child.

I will love you completely all the days of your life.

I have wounds from men. You have wounds from men. (And let's be clear, we have wounded our share of men as well.) But we have a God who serves as our Husband, heavenly Father, and Counselor, who leads us out into the desert and desires to speak tenderly to us and bring us the fullest of healings (Hosea 2:14), and so . . . we will let him.

A Prayer

"Merciful Healer, enter those deep, dark places from which my hurtfulness has come. Touch my hidden wounds, awaken me, set me free, empower me with your new life, enfold me in your mercy. I pray you also heal and enfold those whom I have hurt. I pray in the strong power of your name." —Flora Slosson Wuellner

A Next Good Step

Come up with your own list of messages received, both bad and good, along with a list of ways God promises to restore your heart.

A Way Forward

Therefore, I will charm her,

and bring her into the desert,

and speak tenderly to her heart. . . .

On that day, says the LORD, you will call me, "My husband," and no longer will you call me, "My Lord." (Hosea 2:14, 16)

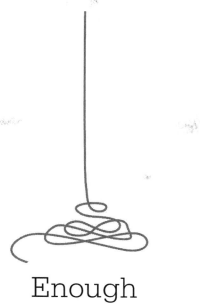

Enough

During my rediscovery of emotional wounds I have collected along the way, specifically from men, one of the main themes that came to the surface was to stop searching the eyes of everybody around me looking for affirmation, looking for who I am, and—to risk a cliché—looking for love.

Words began rising to the surface in this quest. Words like *abide. Rest. Quiet. Peace. Be still and know. Enough.*

Henri Nouwen says that "you are being asked to trust that God is enough for you." I read these words—words so perfectly timed that they could only be God speaking directly to me—and I realize that I need to ask God to help me actually *feel* that he is enough for me. And on the flip side, that who I am is enough for him too.

God offers us a gift of salvation and enough-ness. (I know that's not a word, but I think it should be.)

God didn't say that salvation is Jesus dying on the cross for us *plus* us flogging ourselves because we keep messing up.

He didn't say that salvation is Jesus dying on the cross for us *plus* running ourselves into the ground doing things for him.

And he didn't say that salvation is Jesus dying on the cross for us *plus* all the nice things we can get other people to say about us and to us.

It's just Jesus. It's only Jesus. Jesus is enough.

We can abide in that love. We can find our true rest there. We can live with a quiet heart even in the middle of hard things. We can experience deep peace, as Ephesians 2:14 says that Christ himself is our peace and Colossians 1:27 says that Christ is in us. *Christ is in us.*

Do we get this? That Christ is actually *in* us? Because he is.

We can be still, deep down, and we can know the love of our Father. We can choose to believe that he is enough for us and that we are enough for him. Just as we are.

We can lay down all our striving. We can pick up his grace and his easy burden. In really practical ways, we can abide in Jesus and allow him to abide in us. Through prayer and confession, through reading his word and listening to him, through being as authentic as we can be within community, through asking him to make us aware of his constant presence with us.

I do need to say that, yes, God created us for human companionship; and, no, Jesus won't literally hold us as we fall asleep at night. That longing may always exist, at least in part, for an unmarried person. But there is so much more of God than we can even imagine, than we even bother tapping into. There's so much more of him than there is of our need.

After going through this journey, I've started praying for two things.

One is to see myself only through God's eyes and to lay down what other people think of me.

Henri Nouwen also says, "Over the years you have allowed the voices that call you to action and great visibility to dominate your life. You still think, even against your own best intuitions, that you need to *do things* and *be seen* in order to follow your vocation. But you are now discovering that God's voice is saying, 'Stay home, and trust that your life will be fruitful even when hidden.'" (Italics added.)

We don't have to do and do and do. We can just be. God's love doesn't ebb and flow based on our calendars and our levels of exhaustion. (I'm *not* saying not to serve. What I am saying, though, is to make sure we're serving out of and because of our relationship with Jesus—not as an attempt to garner his affection or make up for our deficits or earn our salvation.)

The other thing I've been praying is that I would trust that God's love is enough for me. One thing I asked myself when I started thinking through my emotional baggage regarding men was, "How do you look Jesus in the eye and tell him that his big, perfect love is great and all, but you're just not sure that it's big enough and perfect enough for you?" Not that I feel God isn't big enough to love me, but I feel as if my neediness is sometimes too big to be filled. So I'm asking God to fill it and then I'm asking him to help me believe that he has, that he can and he will. And I'm asking him to keep me from filling it myself with smaller, fragile things; to instead fill me up with more of him.

A Prayer

Spirit, some days you don't fill me up. I know this is my fault and not yours. I know it's because I'm not seeing things clearly. I know that you are enough for me, enough for me in my pain, enough for me in my healing. But I need you to help me truly feel it and believe it. Be my enough, even if it's just for today. And then I'll ask you again tomorrow. Amen.

A Next Good Step

Are you tired? You can rest. You can stop. You can ask Jesus to renew you. You can be healed and filled up and restored and brought back to life.

Are you trying to live out each day in your own strength? You can abide. You can live out your days in God's strength. Life will still be hard, but you will only bear much fruit if you are abiding in Christ, according to John 15.

Are you running and running to earn your salvation (even if you wouldn't call it that)? It's already earned. It's done. Salvation is Jesus alone. Not Jesus plus anything else.

Do you struggle to feel loved completely, just for you who you are?

You can ask the Spirit to let truth sink into you . . . truth like "you are precious and honored in my sight and I love you."

You can remind yourself that his grace is enough and it's all you need, as we're told in 2 Corinthians 12.

You can remind yourself that your Maker is your husband (Isaiah 54).

You can remind yourself that Jesus is always with you, as he tells us in Matthew 28.

A Way Forward

"Be still, and know that I *am* God." (Psalm 46:10 NKJV)

When you whispered to me to keep my eyes on you because it was only going to get harder, I didn't want to believe you.

Now I do.

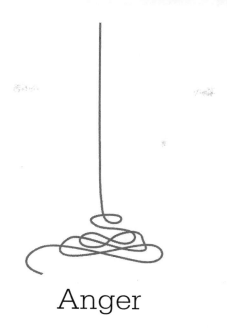

Anger

I am a mad woman, and you can take that any way you want. I have been angry about almost everything there is to be angry about. And I dragged my anger right into my dating relationship with my now-ex-husband, reassuring myself that it was a good sign if I felt comfortable enough with him that I could yell at him so much. I unleashed my anger on him over a four-year courtship and calmed down, somehow, during our first year of marriage.

But then the honeymoon wore off and I found myself constantly listing his faults—how he was letting me down—either mentally or out loud at him. I even got to a place of raging, up to a couple of times a week. I would feel controlled or let down by him, and I would lose my temper; but he would not lose his, and I would find myself lying on my bed with the adrenaline draining out of me. I would cry and beg God to heal me and stop me from doing that again. Repeat cycle. This went on for a couple of years.

I am relieved to say that my anger does not control me the way it used to. I'm sure there are a few factors that go into that—I'm over forty now and not twenty-something. . . . Age and time have mellowed me. I've read books and received counseling and worked on this with all I've got. The Holy Spirit is still working in me after all these years to pull the anger out of me or tamp it down. And then, well, the main recipient of my anger does not live with me anymore, so that cannot help but contribute to my sense of calm.

I have lived too long and been a Christian too long to have still been so infantile when it came to handling my anger. A mother of two and a wife of fifteen-plus years should not be yelling several times a day, at anyone, about anything. Over the years, I made innumerable amends to my then-husband, and still sometimes have to. I've made tearful apologies to my children for modeling such embarrassing, immature behavior. I've also told God how sorry I am, and continue to beg him to take this out of me. Memorizing Scripture, reminding myself constantly that "a fool gives full vent to [her] anger, but a wise [woman] keeps [herself] under control" (Proverbs 29:11 NIV) also has helped tremendously.

But here's what has helped the most: if you find yourself angry all the time, especially right now, make a list of everything that angers you in this tough stretch of life, and then re-read your list. How many of those things are actually sources of fear, sadness or loneliness for you? How many of those things, if you're honest with yourself, are you expressing with hurtful words and impatience and door-slamming when in essence what you're doing is pushing down a floodgate of tears and pain? Anger is cooler. Anger is more justifiable. Anger brings a release. But anger can also be a red flag that waves maniacally over a hurt that you're trying to pretend isn't there. Pretending won't make it go away; it only puts off the inevitable.

A Prayer

"O God, you have bound us together in a common life. Help us, in the midst of our struggles for justice and truth, to confront one another without hatred or bitterness, and to work together with mutual forbearance and respect; through Jesus Christ our Lord. Amen." —*Book of Common Prayer*

A Next Good Step

If anger is not your thing, that's fabulous and be thankful. But if you struggle with anger, pull out that list from above, and add one gratitude next to each item that infuriates or hurts you, asking God to give you a new perspective. Then, add an action step, something that you can do next time in response to the situation that upsets you most consistently.

An example: I hate that my husband has the checkbook in his possession.

Gratitude: I'm grateful we have money in our checking account.

Action step: Now that I'm separated, I'll open a checking account of my own and start setting some money aside.

Seeing things through God's eyes and doing what you can about your circumstances will lessen your feelings of helplessness and, therefore, frustration.

A Way Forward

"Know this, my dear brothers and sisters: everyone should be quick to listen, slow to speak, and slow to grow angry." (James 1:19)

I woke up this morning and realized that, for the first time, I had allowed myself to use the entire bed to sleep, not just my little side. I smiled, and then just as quickly realized how sad that made me feel.

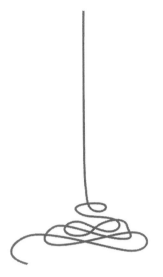

Brokenness

I'm finding that there are all kinds of "broken" in this world:

When you are broken by your own sin.

When you are broken at the hands—or words, or abandoning—of another person.

When you are broken by circumstances.

Or just plain broken, like everybody else.

We are all broken. We all come into this world with the sins of our fathers passed down to us, torn up inside by original sin, but also—gratefully—bearing the image of God. You may look around and feel like the only broken one, but what that probably means is that you're the most authentic one. (If someone seems unbroken, that person is just a master at covering up the truth.)

Life is hard and constantly throws sharp objects at us. We are broken each time we suffer a loss or rejection. Every time we receive scary news from the doctor, get into a car accident, lose a job, or disappoint our child, we break a little bit more.

People can break our hearts. Lies are told. Betrayals are uncovered. Addictions spin out of control. Lovers are taken on the side. Our hearts shatter into millions of pieces and we wonder if we'll ever fully recover.

We make choices. We think bad thoughts, say wrong things, do what we shouldn't do, time and time again. And then comes the moment of truth: will we walk on as if nothing ever happened? Or will we look our sin in the eye and tip our hats, realizing that we were beat, finally admitting that we were not able to stay in control? If we choose to simply move on, we'll never understand redemption. But if we choose honesty and tell the world how we messed up, we will have the opportunity to be broken. Yes, the *opportunity*. God says that he chooses to grant the gift of repentance (2 Timothy 2:24-26 NIV). And it is a gift. A horribly painful and humbling gift, but a gift nonetheless. Because nothing short of recognizing your own sin places you squarely at the foot of the cross where you remember—or realize for the very first time—your rightful place in this world.

"The LORD is close to the brokenhearted; / he saves those whose spirits are crushed" (Psalm 34:18). Is this you today? Is your heart broken? Mine is as I write this. Cling to the reassurance that God moves in even closer to you in these moments, in seasons like these. I can attest to that.

God is sad when we are sad. He carries us during our sorrow. He saves us over and over again. And the best part: he takes our broken pieces and redeems them into something even better than they were before. Hard to imagine, perhaps, but it's true. . . . I've seen it again and again in my life.

You will learn to breathe again. You will one day walk through the halls of your home and no longer be afraid. You will feel one day soon that your dignity has been restored. You will get to a place of not needing to search the eyes of every person in the room for validation that you're OK. You will not always limp through life.

I've heard it said that "hurt people hurt people," but I'd like to then also believe that *broken people—who allow God's healing in—can help people*. No matter what kind of broken you are today—and you are some kind of broken—you can heal. And someday, you can help heal others too.

A Prayer

God, there's no getting around it . . . I am broken. I bear your image but I am a mess. Gladly, I'm *your* mess. Today, please begin a deep healing in me that I can feel and that is evident to those around me. Amen.

A Next Good Step

If you haven't already, it's time to find someone to walk alongside you, be it a mentor, a counselor, or a support group. You cannot heal fully in isolation.

A Way Forward

"The Lord is close to the brokenhearted; / he saves those whose spirits are crushed." (Psalm 34:18)

My children were just picked up again, as happens every other Friday afternoon. I shut the door behind them. The truck pulls away, with a little bit of my heart in the backseat.

My heart feels hollow, not so much out of anticipatory missing of them, although I will, but because this new routine is just that, a routine. A part of our lives now. We made some choices along the way that have brought us to this place.

They say it gets better, but right now I just don't know. The redundant good-byes are killing me.

It's snowing a full, heavy snow and I won't fall asleep knowing that my babies are just a few steps away tonight. It seems colder when they're not here.

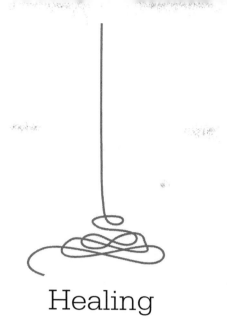

Healing

I have spent my life running hard and fast after healing. I have felt broken, not quite right, just left of center, for as long as I can remember. But I've always looked at healing as something that comes after the fact. You break your leg . . . you get it set . . . it stays in a cast . . . time goes by . . . it heals. Ravi Zacharias in *Cries of the Heart* says, "I used to think that time was a healer. . . . I now believe that time is only the revealer of how God does the healing."

I have come to believe that healing can occur in the middle of the pain. I believe that because I have seen God do so in my life. If I had to wait until my marriage situation were completely wrapped up to find any healing for my heart and soul, I would still be in the fetal position in some dark room somewhere. We all would be. So I have determined—and believe to be true—that God does not wait until you're all the way through something to begin the deep healing work. I so appreciate that.

I've been thinking about resuscitation and resurrection. I've been thinking about how subtly different they are. I've been thinking about what Jesus did. I've been thinking about what I desperately need.

To *resuscitate* means to revive from unconsciousness.

Resurrection is the act of rising from the dead.

I heard Pastor Shane Hipps when he was at Mars Hill Bible Church make this additional distinction between the two. "*Resuscitation*," he said, "brings the person back to their original state, whereas *resurrection* brings the person back transformed."

Every single day, I need little resuscitations. I constantly need to be revived in my physical state, so I sleep, I drink a smoothie or some tea, I take a walk, I breathe in deeply. I continually need to be revived in my parenting, so that I'm consistent, strong, patient, yet gentle . . . all so that I have the energy to remember that I am choosing the harder role of mother first over the easier role of friend. And I most definitely need to be revived in my emotional life, as lately I'm allowing sadness to be my guide.

Oh, but what I need so very much more is resurrection of my soul. There is a dying going on in my life, along with the accompanying grieving. Yet, along with those things comes a promise that there is new life on the other side. The other side for me might be years away, I don't know, but there is another side. I will not remain dead. [I will not even remain "mostly dead," to quote *The Princess Bride*.]

The healing has already begun. I do not cry in the grocery store anymore. I do not cry myself to sleep anymore; well, hardly anymore. I don't mumble when I take out the recycling or when I update the online budget or when I change an outside lightbulb in winter. In fact, I revel a bit in these newfound responsibilities. I don't send twenty e-mails a day to my mentor anymore. I now just send, maybe, five. I don't wear pajamas to every function. I actually get dressed most days. Well, some days. Although I am still a bit more tired than is typical for me, and perhaps in a bit deeper of a melancholy funk, my energy is returning, as is my creativity and my joy.

In part, I'm sure, it's because I have chosen every day a hundred times to do the thing that's in front of me, even when I didn't want to do it. There's a popular saying in recovery that says, "When I got busy, I got better." So much of the daily work of healing your soul will come in getting out of bed and putting clothes on and then, you know, running an errand or making sure you eat something, anything.

But the main component of my healing as I meander through is God's grace. "As for you, I'll come with healing, / curing the incurable" (Jeremiah 30:17 *THE MESSAGE*).

He comes with healing—present-tense *comes*. He comes to us. He bends down to us. He wipes away our tears. He wraps us up in his arms. He brings a restoration and revival.

Remember that healing is a process, not a one-time event. We cannot possibly be fully healed from the pain we're experiencing right now because it's not over yet. There will be a full healing someday. So I wait for my personal resurrection, I long for it. I hold on to the hope of the transformation that will accompany it, but I also hope for something even better: that the one who is my Resurrector is all-knowing, all-seeing, all-loving and himself a resurrected one, so he knows what he's doing in me.

A Prayer

"Spirit of comfort and longing, enfold my fear, unclothe me of my pride, unweave my thoughts, uncomplicate my heart, and give me surrender: that I may tell my wounds, lay down my work, and greet the dark." —Janet Morley

A Next Good Step

Healing work will require willingly bringing into your life a slower pace. The Spirit's work on your heart cannot be hurried, the mending work of a soul cannot be rushed. You cannot be excessively busy and heal at the same time . . . and frankly, I don't think you would want to. So ask God if there's anything in your life that you can lay aside for a season, so that you may focus more fully on your current situation.

A Way Forward

"God heals the brokenhearted / and bandages their wounds." (Psalm 147:3)

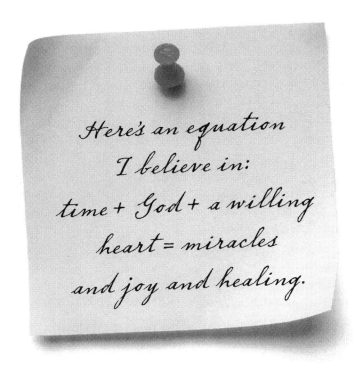

Here's an equation I believe in: time + God + a willing heart = miracles and joy and healing.

Suffering

I 've read enough books on suffering and pain during my life-time that I could probably have my doctorate by now. And three theories have bubbled up to the surface for me that help me frame my personal suffering in tangible terms.

First, I've heard it said that suffering only truly counts once you begin handling it correctly. All suffering before that is simply a shame and a waste. To be clear, all suffer-ing is messy and uncomfortable, but there are different ways to handle it. Although my marriage-suffering was punctuated with pleas to God for help throughout the years, in some ways I didn't suffer well. In the early years, although I asked for help, I didn't keep asking for help until I got it, and I didn't keep asking until I felt truly heard. I kept much of the pain to myself. I kept our secret—that we weren't the perfect little family—for much too long, in large part out of pride, out of a concern for what other people would think of me if they knew the truth. I filled my time with other things so I wouldn't have to think about the pain so much. I blamed my husband and refused to look at my part in our situation. But I realize now that it was only once I brought the whole truth out into the light, and began to work on myself, that my suffering started to be handled the way it should be, that it started to count for something.

Second, we should not be surprised by our suffering. I feel shocked each time something even remotely bad happens to me or to my friends. But I shouldn't be. I said to a friend recently, "Is it my imagination, or do our lives seem harder sometimes simply because we're Christians?" I already knew the answer, but it helps to hear it come from someone else from time to time. And she replied, resoundingly, "Yes! I wish we didn't have to think about two-thirds of the things we have to think about. And of course, we have an enemy." Oh yeah, I keep forgetting that part. I keep forgetting that Jesus said, "In the world you have distress" (John 16:33). We are promised trouble and should live with a gentle expectation of it.

And then there's what Peter tells us: "Instead, rejoice as you share Christ's suffering. You share his suffering now so that you may also have overwhelming joy when his glory is revealed" (1 Peter 4:13).

I've heard it said that while Christ is preparing a place for you and me, the Holy Spirit is preparing us to meet Jesus face to face, and it's our trials that complete and prepare us.

There is a reason that our lives may at times feel harder than those who don't even think about God. Much needs to be accomplished in us to prepare us for meeting God. And that takes time and patience and working things out in ways that we can't even fathom here and now. But here's where faith comes in because we must choose to believe that whatever we go through here and now, it will be so very worth it there and then.

And lastly, you can either waste your pain or you can allow Jesus to use your pain. I don't know if it's my melancholy bent, but there is something about being in a dark stretch of life that resonates with my soul and wakes it up to spiritual things in ways that skipping through life on a sunny day just never does. The professional struggle that I went through several years ago brought evidence all over my life of how God changed me to my core during that hard time. But I don't think he would have—at least not to the extent that he did—had I not been willing. I begged him to teach me and change me, and he sweetly obliged. What a shame it would've been had I gone through all of that only to have my life and my heart look exactly the same at the end as it had when the trouble started. And because I saw up close how gracious God is in keeping his promise to redeem every single moment of hurt that enters my life, I am now much quicker to ask him to work in me through stretches of difficulty. And now is no exception.

We may have little to no control over circumstances that bring suffering into our lives, but we can control how we respond to it. Will we waste our suffering or will we suffer well? It's our choice.

A Prayer

Redeemer, please use this time in my life to bring forth beauty from ashes. Do not let me waste my suffering. Help me experience your comfort deeply so I can one day pour it out into someone else who is hurting. Amen.

A Next Good Step

So allow me to encourage you—as someone who has suffered incorrectly and as someone who has seen the deep good of allowing God to put a purpose to my pain. You can just throw the pain out, but you will deeply regret it if you do. So, use this time to work on yourself. Get a counselor, get into a recovery group, whatever you need. But do not let yourself believe the lie that you are where you are solely because of your ex-spouse and that you have nothing to learn. Let your suffering count for something.

A Way Forward

The LORD God's spirit is upon me,
>because the LORD has anointed me.

He has sent me
>to bring good news to the poor,
>to bind up the brokenhearted,
>to proclaim release for captives,
>and liberation for prisoners, . . .
>to provide for Zion's mourners,
>to give them a crown in place of ashes,
>oil of joy in place of mourning,
>a mantle of praise in place of discouragement.

(Isaiah 61:1, 3)

*I feel surrounded today,
in a good way,
with peace and quietness
and a gentle,
lingering love.*

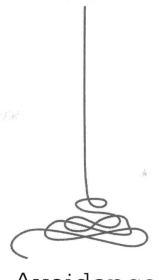

Avoidance

If a tree falls in the forest and there's no one there to hear it or see it fall, did it really fall? Or in our terms, if a marriage is falling apart but no one else is present to witness it from the inside, is it really falling apart? I would have always answered yes to the tree question and no to the marriage question.

I was the woman who didn't want to admit—to anyone, including herself—that everything was falling apart. I was the woman who thought the husband, house, large amounts of church commitment, and two children would paint over her reality and keep everyone fooled—including herself. I was the woman who didn't want to believe what was really happening: that her marriage was fragile, thin, breaking into a million pieces, completely out of her control.

I thought if I had all of the outside trappings, and read all the right books, and said all the right words, and joined all the right groups, and talked to all the right counselors, and prayed all the right prayers, and just stayed and stayed and stayed that I could avoid the truth. Make it go away. Change it. Heal it, even.

Avoidance is the act of keeping something away, pretending it's not real. I was shunning my bad marriage. I told it that it wasn't welcome in my home, my family, my life. But it set up shop early on and lingered in the background of my every move, my every day, my every thought. Hands down, no matter how busy I was raising my children, starting up ministries, leading teams, highlighting a cause, traveling to developing countries, working at church, writing books, speaking at women's events, I always had as my number-one focus my difficult marriage. It has been my addiction, my obsession, dare I say my idol. And yet, I avoided my truth because my truth was too hard to enfold into my life. My sweet little Jesus-loving, Jesus-serving life didn't have room for that truth. I never really felt that I could fully love Jesus and be in a bad marriage at the same time—and I desperately wanted to fully love Jesus—so I pretended everything was just fine, proudly wearing the mask to much of the outside world. But everything wasn't fine.

What I've learned is this. You can avoid the truth for a very,

very long time, but it will come out. And if you try to stuff the truth down, it will come out all sideways and wonky and when you are least prepared.

So, come to terms with your truth now. You're separated or divorced—that means something went deeply wrong in your relationship with your spouse. Don't run away from that. Use this time to look at it from all angles, to look at it full in the face. It's time to stop avoiding.

A Prayer

Lord, open my eyes and allow me to see my marriage as you see it. Show me what I need to see, but please hold my hand and bring people around me to soften the blow, as the truth frightens me to my core right now. Amen.

A Next Good Step

Get out your journal and define your reality, even if it hurts to see it in print. Tell yourself as much of the truth right now as your heart can hold, even if it's just a recounting of yesterday's argument or how lonely the nights are. If it ends up being too raw, enjoy the experience of shredding it or tucking it away in the bottom of a drawer for another time.

A Way Forward

"Since God has so generously let us in on what he is doing, we're not about to throw up our hands and walk off the job just because we run into occasional hard times. We refuse to wear masks and play games. We don't maneuver and manipulate behind the scenes. And we don't twist God's Word to suit ourselves. Rather, we keep everything we do and say out in the open, the whole truth on display, so that those who want to can see and judge for themselves in the presence of God." (2 Corinthians 4:1-2 *THE MESSAGE*)

I had just endured a three-hour argument that was filled with sobbing, accusations, and much pleading. There was no level below this. I had finally hit bottom. I knew that I would never go back to "us." It was over. I was finished. Sometimes the only way we can move into our future is to burn down our past. And sometimes the only way we can have the courage to do that is when we've been so torn to pieces, so destroyed, that there is nothing left to repair, that there is no way to put back together all that's disintegrated. I've never been so broken in my entire life. I've never been so scared.

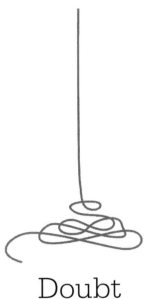

Doubt

Being separated or divorced is a perpetual state of confusion and questions. *What did I do wrong? Was there anything I could've done differently? Did my husband ever love me? Were we wrong to separate? Am I completely incapable of being in a healthy relationship? Will he come back? Do I want him to come back? What does my future hold? What does God want for me? Will I be taken care of? Will I make it through this? Will this mess up my kids or my testimony or my life forever?*

Doubt hums in the background. Doubt follows you around. I remember standing in the grocery store at the beginning of my separation, dazed and confused, frozen with indecision in front of a row of cereals. I almost started to cry. I berated myself, *You can't even handle picking a cereal? How are you going to get through this thing?*

I struggled with doubt throughout my entire marriage. *Should we have gotten married? Am I as incompetent as I've been made to feel? Are we going to make it? Am I doomed to replicate what I grew up with? Is this all in my head? Is this normal? Do other couples fight like this, fight this much? Will I always feel this lonely, like this much of a failure? What if I make the wrong decision now? Will I ruin everything?*

But probably my largest sense of doubt has surrounded who I think God is. You see, I spent years and years begging God to heal this broken-down relationship. And then I watched it get progressively worse while I became progressively more sad and closed off. It's hard to pray for something for a really, really long time and infer that God's response is either a *no* or a *not yet* for so many years. Clearly, he didn't respond with a yes, or I wouldn't be here.

But the doubt loomed larger because it's not as if the thing I was praying for all that time was, you know, a yacht or a boyfriend. I was asking for something that I was pretty sure God would have wanted for us: a restored, whole marriage between two people who claimed to love him. How could he not want that for us?

So what I came to doubt was God's will. And his plan. And even his intentions toward those who are his. Didn't he love me? Did he really want me to be this sad, this desperate, this lonely for the rest of my life? Did he really want this marriage to serve as my children's model?

To be honest, I still do not have the answers to most of those questions. I'm OK with that, for one reason. Scripture is clear that his ways are higher than my ways, and over the years I have not only come to accept but to celebrate that if I could fully understand God, he wouldn't be the kind of God who would deserve my worship.

Gratefully, I have one answer that carries me through the rest of the unanswerables. God's intentions toward me *are* good and pure, and God *does* love me. Those are steady posts in a life driven by circumstance. And when I'm filled with doubt, when I'm standing in the grocery store wondering if I can choose a cereal, I can remember the only thing that is sure, the only thing I really need to know: *I am loved.*

A Prayer

Jesus, there is so much ambiguity and uncertainty swirling through my life right now. Every choice feels huge and every decision feels wrong. I'm on shaky ground in my circumstances, but I want to be steady deep down in my soul. Remind me that you are my strong tower and that I can run to you for permanent shelter. Amen.

A Next Good Step

Jot down your current questions and doubts. You may be surprised how many concerns you are actually carrying around with you every day. Then ask God to begin to answer each of those questions in your life, in ways that you can understand.

A Way Forward

"At that the boy's father cried out, 'I have faith; help my lack of faith!'" (Mark 9:24)

Raw today.

Strength

With tears in her eyes, she said to me, "You were always the strong one." I let those words brush past me in the moment, knowing they'd come crashing back on me later. A dear friend said this to me. She didn't mean an ounce of harm; in fact, she meant it as the highest of compliments. The context was my separation, and she was reminiscing about how I used to be the one she would come to with her marriage struggles because she knew I'd understand. In fact, for about six months, she and another dear friend and I were getting together every couple of weeks to go through a book study and encourage one another in our faith walks but mostly in our difficult marriages. I used to say to them at the end of our time together, "But we're all still married. We stayed married one more day, girls! That counts for something!" And we'd kind of laugh and hug, but we knew those words were true as we'd all walk back into our hard situations.

But back to me no longer being the strong one. This implies to me that I was either healthier back then or less authentic than I thought I was . . . or worse yet, that I'm just plain weaker now.

And I just might be. I am feeling super fragile these days. Vulnerable. Kind of dried up. A bit listless. As if I could blow away in a strong wind if I'm not careful. I'm being encouraged to serve Jesus in the meantime, to wring this season dry of every lesson that God has for me. And I want to do those things. In fact, in other hard life stretches, I would've been the poster girl for soldiering on and lesson-gleaning. Now I'm the poster girl for dark under-eye circles. Or the benefits of napping. Or wearing pajamas in public. So perhaps I am less strong. Or perhaps these things are justified as this is a slow death of my most important relationship, and that surely takes a lot out of a girl.

But I have been told that how I handled my marriage and how I am handling the dissolution of my marriage both show a lack of strength. I've been told that I should be kicking butt. I've been told that I don't stack up to other women who would be handling this situation differently (read *better*). I've been told, "I guess we're just different. I'm strong, independent . . ." (which implies that *I'm* not).

My friend's words crippled me in the moment, but then I really sat with them. And now I beg to differ.

I know what it took to stay married for six thousand-plus days when the marriage was breaking apart. I know what it took to stay put, trying to give my children the stability that I didn't have growing up. I know what it took, struggling to keep my vows to stay when pretty much every day found me praying for an out. That's not cowardice. That's not being a wimp who was afraid to leave. I stayed out of intent, not out of weakness or fear.

And I know what it has taken to get through this season of disentangling myself from my ex-husband, a process that is still going on and will continue for a few more years, from what I'm told. I've had time to let the idea settle in, but that doesn't mean I didn't feel as if I'd been kicked in the gut when I saw his signature on the divorce papers. It doesn't mean I'm used to the idea that I might be alone for the rest of my life.

I may have cried a lot and worn my pajamas for days on end and forgotten to eat from time to time, but that isn't weakness. It's called grieving.

My choices and decisions may have left some people scratching their heads, but those people aren't me. And they haven't lived my life. And they don't know my heart.

I know that my intention through every day of almost three decades has been to follow God. When I have broken his heart, mine has broken too. When I chose to walk away from my marriage, even though advised to do so, I did so with sadness and regret.

And yet I also did so with strength. Enduring a difficult marriage and then walking away because it's the best thing to do, all while trying to raise two children—all while knowing many people will disapprove of you—is not for the weak.

There is a strength that accompanies those who wait on the Lord, who do what's right no matter how hard (staying, then leaving, in my case), who don't worry themselves with the opinions of others.

I may appear weak and foolish, but if my true strength comes from God, then frankly I'm stronger than I even know. In fact, in some small ways, I feel emotionally stronger than I ever have felt. I am a cross between I-am-woman-hear-me-roar and Lord-lead-me-through-this-refining-fire. I have never stood up for myself in quite the ways that I have in recent years, and yet I don't feel the least bit selfish but instead completely supported by Jesus. He didn't want me treated the way I was treated. I believe he didn't like it when I was told not to get too worked up about the way I was treated.

Which means right now, I believe that he is pleased that I am walking in truth, that the light has been shed on my secret life. I believe he is holding me. I believe he is more than OK with me struggling through all this, because really, this is huge. I believe he is allowing my strength to wane just a bit because he knows what I forget—that when I am weak, he is the most strong.

So, I'm not the strong one I used to be—or maybe never was—but I am wiser. And I am covered over in a bigger, tougher, yet gentler strength that will carry me through whatever may be just around the bend.

A Prayer

"Lord Jesus, our Savior, let us come to you. Our hearts are cold; Lord, warm them with your selfless love. Our hearts are sinful; cleanse them with your precious blood. Our hearts are weak; strengthen them with your joyous Spirit. Our hearts are empty; fill them with your divine presence. Lord Jesus, our hearts are yours; possess them always and only for yourself."
—St. Augustine of Hippo (354–430)

A Next Good Step

Recount a time in your life when you felt stronger emotionally and a time when you felt like an emotional wreck. In which season did you experience God more intimately, and why?

A Way Forward

"He said to me, 'My grace is enough for you, because power is made perfect in weakness.'" (2 Corinthians 12:9)

Today I don't wait without hope. I wait knowing. I can know that all will come to pass, that all will be made right, that I am being saved each and every day, that I will one day walk completely healed and whole, that I will one day stop having this feeling of yearning and of lack because it will all be OK.

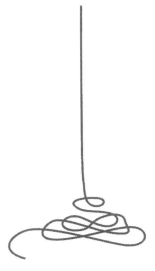

Sadness

Confession number one: my very favorite place in the world right now is in my bed with the heating blanket on.

Confession number two: my very favorite thing to do in the world right now is sleep.

Confession number three: I am depressed.

I don't know if it's clinical, chemical, circumstantial, seasonal, or a combination of all of the above. I don't even know if there's a difference between all those. And I really don't think it matters. But I know that I am depressed.

I am sad. I am tired. It's winter here as I write. The holidays are long gone, but a blizzard just hit a few days ago. It feels as though spring will never arrive, literally and figuratively. There is a malaise that is hanging over me. I yelled loudly in my bathroom just yesterday, "I'm tired of being sad! I'm tired of in-between!" (No worries, I was home alone.) I also cried along with—and I mean sob-cried—an Air Supply song. That should pretty much put the nail in any coffin of doubt about my current mental state. (*"I'm all out love; I'm so lost without you. . . ."* You try singing that without a tear or two forming.)

Here's the worst part about this: I feel purposeless. The last time I was not serving in some active capacity was— well, before I became a Christ-follower almost thirty years ago. In this current season, I am doing nothing to help anyone else, so it seems. (I do not count parenting, sending the occasional note to a friend, praying the occasional extra prayer for someone, or blogging as "Christian service"; but it sure would be great if God did. Then again, maybe he does.)

I have lived for so long as a Type-A, anal-retentive, controlling overachiever. In the past two decades, I've had two children, written seven books, started a speaking ministry, started and led the women's ministry at my church, joined the staff of my church as part-time adult ministry director, started the AIDS team at my church, joined the board of directors at my local AIDS clinic, and traveled to three third-world countries. However, within the past year, I have served in children's ministry once, for an hour. And I think that's about it.

That is so sad to me. I used to feel so full of life. (Or, truth be told, perhaps I was trying to *appear* full of life.) And right now, life is being sucked out of me. This fact is also hugely guilt-inducing for me. Are my most productive years behind me? Is it all downhill from here already? Will I never again have something of value to offer someone else? I'm only in my forties.

The upside to this sadness, I hope, is that my children will see me honestly dealing with my feelings and authentically running to Jesus for help, healing, and comfort. I hope they know that Jesus is my absolute best friend. I know I'm not alone. I know Jesus loves me. I am not hopeless, as my eternity is secure and my Peace *is* Christ. But I'm still sad, and I fear everyone can tell just by looking at me.

And yet, I'm reminded of something I used to hear a friend say quite often: "This is only a season." Ecclesiastes reminds us that there is a time for pretty much everything, and right now just might be our time for sadness. But just as surely as this time has swept into our lives, it will roll right back out; and we will find ourselves waking up, feeling a sense of spring deep down in our bones, and looking up and out just like we used to, maybe even stronger than before. Singer/songwriter Audrey Assad sings, "Even the winter won't last forever / we'll see the morning, we'll feel the sun." Only this time, we'll have a deeper well of experience to draw from as we look for someone else to serve, as we look for a way to turn our seasons of sadness into a harvest of good. There is a purpose to this melancholia, and Jesus—the keeper of our soul and the holder of our tears—will reveal it to us when the time is right.

A Prayer

[O Lord,] my soul breaks with longing
for Your judgments at all times. . . .
My soul clings to the dust;
revive me according to Your word. . . .
My soul melts from heaviness;
strengthen me according to Your word. . . .
Remember the word to Your servant,
upon which You have caused me to hope.
This *is* my comfort in my affliction,
for Your word has given me life.
[Amen.]
(Psalm 119:20, 25, 28, 49-50 NKJV)

A Next Good Step

If you find yourself in a sad place today, make a list of the reasons why you're troubled. Then say each reason out loud to God, asking him to carry it for you for just this day. If you're in an OK place today, though, make a list of ten activities you enjoy doing that can help pull you out of your funk the next time the blues roll in.

A Way Forward

There is a time for everything,
> and a season for every activity under heaven:
>> . . . a time to weep,
>> . . . a time to mourn. (Ecclesiastes 3:1, 4 NIV)

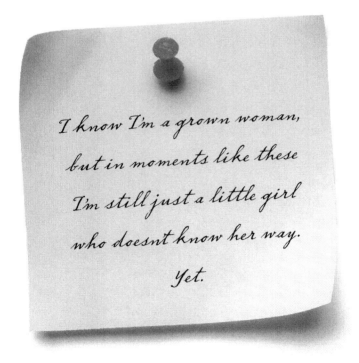

I know I'm a grown woman, but in moments like these I'm still just a little girl who doesnt know her way.

Yet.

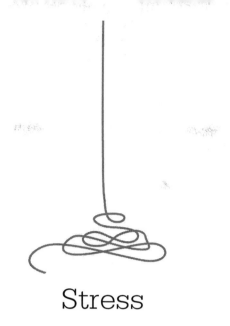

Stress

I am no longer an overly busy woman, for which I am extremely grateful. I had a season in my life when I was on staff part-time at my church while trying to raise my kids and run my home and write a book and build a speaking career. At some point, I felt completely overwhelmed—as if my life were living me instead of the other way around—but I kept on rolling along. I just kept pushing through and doing all of the things I had been doing. But not anymore. Now I am a stay-at-home mom to two teenagers. I have the writing and speaking career but also some time to just be. It's a sweeter, quieter, slower-paced life, and I am thankful.

But being divorced means a few things. It means that I am on dinner duty every night. It means I take the recycling to the end of the driveway on Tuesday evenings. It means I'm the one to take both kids to school and get them to and from youth group and basketball practice and basketball games and driver's ed class and anything else they want or need to do. It means I'm the one who does the "we ran out of milk" runs instead of texting a spouse to pick some up on the way home from work. It means I write the tithe checks and weed the flower bed and get the dead mice off the patio and change my printer cartridge and buy the dog food and put both kids to bed each night and make the decisions and lay down the law, on my own, every day and every night. It's all on my shoulders now.

The dailiness of doing this alone is wearing. The breaks come only in fragments. I'm the good cop *and* the bad cop. The stress of having to remember everything on my own, even as the organized person I am, can sometimes be too much. I forget that the oil needs changing and that I was supposed to take the kids back to the dentist. There's no one to remind me of these things, or to ask me how it's going at the end of the day.

My daughter had a cold sore recently, and my son asked her what it was and how you get one. She told him, "I think it's usually from stress," to which my son said, "Then why doesn't Mom have one every day of her life?" *Nice.* Apparently, I'm stressed and it's no secret.

Being on my own, I've realized that I cannot do it all, that I do not *have* to do it all. That some things are just going to fall through the cracks, and that's what grace is for. That I have to be intentional about getting my emotional, spiritual and physical cup filled up so I'll have what it takes to stay calm and pour out into my kids, at least most of the time.

I do this by knowing myself well. I literally have a list written down of what I love to do, things I'd love to try, ways that I connect best with God, and then I make sure I'm doing those things. I set dates with friends. I joined a Bible study specifically to get me through this season. I take walks to pray and think. I sometimes do yoga, I journal, I read. It's so important for me not to give my children, my friends, and the world around me the worst parts of me, the tired parts, the stressed parts, the burned-to-the-ground parts. I want them to have the quiet parts, the strong parts, the calm parts. But it won't just happen on its own.

A Prayer

Hear my prayer, O LORD,
and let my cry come to You.
Do not hide Your face from me in the day of my trouble;
incline Your ear to me;
in the day that I call, answer me speedily.
For my days are consumed like smoke,
and my bones are burned like a hearth.
My heart is stricken and withered like grass. . . .

My days are like a shadow that lengthens,
and I wither away like grass.
But You, O LORD, shall endure forever. . . .
[Amen.]
(Psalm 102:1-4, 12 NKJV)

A Next Good Step

Dream a little bit. Is there a list of movies that you've been wanting to watch? Rent them from the library. A part of town you've always wanted to explore? Go there and spend an afternoon around new places and sounds and people. A trip you want to take? Start saving up. Make your own list and start filling yourself up.

A Way Forward

"Be careful and stay calm. Don't fear, and don't lose heart." (Isaiah 7:4)

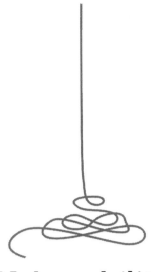

Vulnerability

I knew I was heading into risky territory when I began checking Facebook to see if I had any new messages from a friend. A guy friend. A married guy friend. My heart would beat a little faster and I'd read and re-read the messages.

And then, in a stronger moment, I wrote him this:

> So I've been thinking. I'm super vulnerable and needy these days. The most recent and substantial contact I had with a man was with the guy who changed my oil a couple of days ago. I should have a sign on my forehead that says "dangerous." I feel like the harlot in Proverbs calling from the

street. You're happily married; I'm miserably divorced. Not a good combination for anyone, but especially not for me. So I think I should take a little break.

He responded graciously and we went our separate Facebook ways.

Me plus *any* man right now is not a good combination. I'm vulnerable. I'm lonely. I'm not fully who I am. I'm rethinking everything. I'm replacing lies with truth. I'm still walking wounded. I'm in the middle of the healing process. I don't know what I *need*, and the things that I *want* wouldn't be good or right for me now.

A little while ago, I was on a walk with my kids and they were up ahead of me. In that moment, without even thinking, I actually felt my hand drift to the side as if I expected a man's hand to be waiting to take hold of mine. In my core, I am missing partnership, physiologically as well as emotionally and spiritually.

And because I know this about myself—that I can be inappropriately flirty in my neediness—I've had to take some steps to guard my heart. The first step, of course, was curtailing that potentially hazardous Facebook communication. I have also made the choice not to work with male editors, publicists, or agents right now. I don't respond to male strangers' Facebook messages (and I've gotten some doozies, I'll tell you). And I'm praying for God's healing and protection over my still-broken heart. I'm not even close to thinking of the possibility of another man being in my life at some point

(I don't know yet if I even want that), so I'm asking God to pretty much just keep men at bay. (It's working so far.)

We are in an exposed place, at these times in our lives. We are susceptible to rebound relationships. I've heard that it takes one year for every four years you were married to come to a place of fairly complete healing; and trust me, we need to heal before we move into another relationship.

This is the perfect time to learn, maybe for the first time, what Isaiah meant when he said, "for your Maker is your husband" (54:5 NIV). No, God does not physically hold us, but there are other, deeper ways that God can minister to us, bless us, heal us, and be our companion, if we let him.

A Prayer

God, I need you in new ways right now. I am wide open. I need your protection over my heart. Help me be wise with who I choose to spend time with and who I let into my life and my heart. Heal me. Soothe me. Teach me to come to you first. And become my Spouse in ways I couldn't have even imagined. Amen.

A Next Good Step

You're not going to like this one. I want you to ask a friend to keep you accountable in this area. She is allowed to ask you anything. And you need to promise yourself that you will tell her the truth. It's for your own protection.

A Way Forward

"Above all else, guard your heart, for everything you do flows from it." (Proverbs 4:23 NIV)

I have never in all my life walked out of church in the middle of worship, but today I did.

It was a perfect storm: Father's Day, my kids not with me, all those grown men choosing to get baptized. . . .

Divorce just keeps sneaking up on me—and kicking me in the gut, and taking my breath away—when I least expect it.

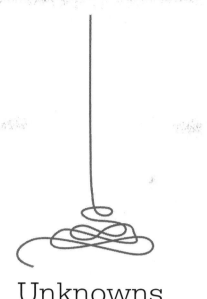

Unknowns

I f you are a woman who has been married for any length of time, you know that you become accustomed to being someone's wife. *Wife* becomes not just a title, not just a role, but a part of who you are. (And, although I don't know from experience, I assume the same can be said for men—*husband* becomes part of who you are.) During my separation, I came to believe that the most fitting title for my marital status was estranged wife. What a lovely term, *estranged*. We are currently disconnected and detached.

There is an unknown that comes with the territory of separation and the process of divorcing. When you are married, even in a difficult marriage, you know you are married. But being in process—being in this no-man's land, pun intended—is full of unknowns. We do not know our future, nor do we know how long it will take for us to arrive at it.

"You don't really know about tomorrow. What is your life? You are a mist that appears for only a short while before it vanishes" (James 4:14). I think we tend to forget that every day is an unknown. That every future is unknown. That the length of every marriage is, technically, unknown.

"Then you will have a future, and your hope won't be cut off" (Proverbs 23:18). This is truly great news for us. We all have a future. We may not know what it holds, but we know that our hope will not end.

If you're anything like me—a control freak—you wrestle with not being able to pin down where you'll be in a year, or in six months: where am I going to live? Or this week: in my emotionally overwhelmed state, will I get this work project done in time? Or tomorrow: what time will my kids be brought home? Or even today: will I get an upsetting voice mail? This kind of not knowing kills me. It has been so harrying at times that on more than one occasion, I've considered bringing on a conclusion of any kind, rushing the hand of God for my own comfort and security.

But today I will rest in knowing that, although my tomorrow has never been truly known by me, it is fully known by God. Our every tomorrow is seen by God right now. Breathe deep—we are in trustworthy, all-seeing hands, no matter what we can't see, no matter what's coming.

A Prayer

"Spirit of Hope, blessed be this new life. Blessed be this new beginning. Blessed be this healing. Blessed be this letting go, and this keeping. Spirit of Hope, blessed be this new life." —a prayer by an unknown author

A Next Good Step

Come up with a list of specific unknowns. Will you and your spouse reconcile, live separated long-term, or divorce? Will you have to move? Will you have to get a different job? Will you have to find a new church? Now surrender each one of these unknowns to God.

A Way Forward

"I'm convinced that nothing can separate us from God's love in Christ Jesus our Lord: not death or life, not angels or rulers, not present things or future things, not powers or height or depth, or any other thing that is created." (Romans 8:38-39)

I think you want me to be more generous—more high-road-ish. Help me act "as if."

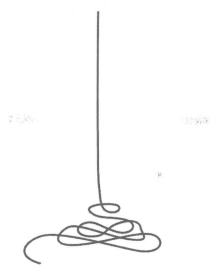

Exhaustion

I met a new friend for tea this morning. We bonded over our natural bent toward sarcasm infused into every other sentence and our fondness for using our exhaustion as an excuse to get out of stuff we don't want to do.

The huge difference between us is that she is pregnant. You know, as in her body is creating another person. So, yeah, she's tired a lot. I, on the other hand, am not creating another person. And yet, I'm tired a lot.

I had a regular day today. I got up, showered, got my kids to school, spent some time with Jesus, met my pregnant friend for tea, ran to Trader Joe's, then Target, then the bank. I went home, put my purchases away, checked e-mail, tried to fix my Quicken software, pulled something out of the freezer for dinner, did a load of laundry, and then realized it was one o'clock in the afternoon and I was tired. So I took a nap. Yep, this forty-something stay-at-home mom whose kids are in school full-time took a nap at one o'clock in the afternoon because she was tired.

What in the world is there to be tired about?

Well, just as my friend is tired because she is creating a person, I am tired because I am dissolving something.

The grief alone could keep me in bed for a year. But then there's the other stuff.

I have been part of a couple for half my life, my entire adulthood. I am learning, for the first time, how to be on my own in every part of my life. I am learning to do everything by myself and have no other adult to bounce things off of or to get advice from.

I had to figure out Quicken today. Not that big of a deal, except that deep down I realize I have to figure out Quicken because I now am in charge of my finances and there is no one else to handle them. Exhausting reminder.

There's looking ahead at the rest of this week and trying to figure out how to be in two places at once, how to get two kids to two separate locations all by myself. Exhausting reminder.

Driving home from Target, I almost headed accidentally to my old house. Exhausting reminder.

Taking my daughter to driver's ed, we passed our old street. Exhausting reminder.

I received an e-mail from my lawyer today about some financial papers I need to look over. Exhausting reminder.

And tonight, it was just three of us having dinner together, again. And it will only be three of us having dinner until my kids move out. Exhausting reminder.

When the kids are picked up by their dad for the weekend, exhausting reminder.

When I get a piece of mail made out to *Ms.* Elisabeth Corcoran, exhausting reminder.

When I get a piece of mail made out to *Mrs.* Elisabeth Corcoran, exhausting reminder.

Every day is filled with reminders that things are completely different. That our reality is not at all what we had planned or hoped for. So yes, I'm exhausted. You are probably exhausted too.

And yes, it is so totally OK to take a nap.

A Prayer

Lord, you are the everlasting God, the creator of the ends of the earth. You don't grow tired or weary. Your understanding is beyond human reach. Please give power to the tired and revive the exhausted. Amen. —based on Isaiah 40:28-29 CEB

A Next Good Step

I talk a lot about naps. Clearly, I'm a fan. One of my friends told me that her pastor several years ago gave her this advice: "Sometimes the most spiritual thing you can do is take a nap." You may not like to nap or don't have the time; but I'm going to challenge you to make sure that you get to bed at a reasonable hour each evening, and start a nighttime routine that prepares your body for a good night's rest. You need this.

A Way Forward

"Come to me, all you who are struggling hard and carrying heavy loads, and I will give you rest." (Matthew 11:28)

Just plain waiting for my next season to start. And there's not one thing I can do to hurry it along.

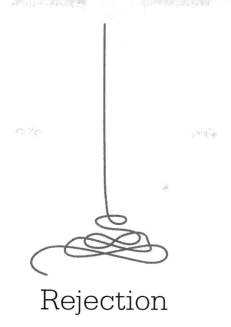

Rejection

I n all my years, I have never been physically hurt by some-one. No one has ever slapped me or punched me or pushed me against a wall. My hair hasn't been pulled, I've gotten no black eyes, and no bones have been broken. I've never been raped. I'm truly beyond thankful for that.

Yet I am no stranger to being flattened out emotionally by someone else. In fact, as I write, I am hollowed out by an excruciatingly difficult few days. I feel as if someone reached inside me, pulled out my heart, and tossed it on the sidewalk.

It puts you in a desolate place, to feel beaten up. To feel as if no one really understands the hurt except you. To feel unprotected. It's especially exhausting when you feel as if the finish line keeps moving a mile farther away, just when you're at your breaking point. It's especially devastating when the clobbering comes from someone you had hoped it would never come from.

I filed a petition for legal separation after much prayer and wise counsel. Weeks went by with not a word regarding my petition. Each time I e-mailed my lawyer, he told me that he'd heard nothing at all.

Then two months after I filed, my lawyer was contacted by my husband's lawyer. My husband had counter-filed, not for legal separation but for dissolution of marriage. The reality of those words didn't sink in too deeply because I knew it wouldn't seem real to me until I had proof that the papers had been filed.

Another month of silence went by. I have come to despise silence.

Then I received an e-mail. Attached to it were divorce papers filed by my husband, and I saw his signature.

For a girl who grew up as a child of divorce, for a girl who convinced herself early on that she would have to beg any man to love her, for a girl who assumed no man would actually stick around for the long haul, this was prophecy fulfilled, the ultimate rejection.

I am being left. In really quiet moments, I believe that it's all my fault—because, bottom line, I feel I am not good enough to be loved. *It's official,* I chide myself, *and I've got the paper-work to prove it.*

I am trying to look for Jesus in all of this, but on my lowest, murkiest days, the closest I get is calling out his name as I try to fall asleep. *Jesus,* I whisper. *Jesus.* I wait for his answer.

A Prayer

"O my Lord—wash me, wash me of this relationship; wash me of the pain of it, wash me of the hurt of it, wash me of the disappointment of it, wash me of the resentment of it, wash me of the attachment to it, wash me of the hurtful memories that come back in quietness, and in prayer, that come back in the silent night hours. I give myself into your hands, Lord. Do for me what I cannot do for myself. Heal me, Lord. Under your healing touch hour by hour, and day by day I shall be set free." —a prayer by an unknown author

A Next Good Step

Make plans to spend time with one of your best friends doing something totally fun. Let yourself feel loved.

A Way Forward

"After all, he has said, *I will never leave you or abandon you.*" (Hebrews 13:5)

Fill me in ways that a husband should, Lord. . . . Honestly, I'm not even sure what I'm asking for.

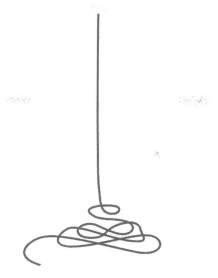

Enemies

When I was a little girl, I knew plenty of other little girls who didn't like me or who made fun of me or whom I didn't like. Even today there are people I would classify as "not having my back"; in that case, I simply keep my emotional distance. But I'm grateful to say that until this point in my life I'd never had what I would consider an enemy.

I try to pray some of those enemy prayers in the Psalms, but I can't seem to bring myself to pray the lines that ask God to destroy a nemesis. I find myself holding on to lifelines like these from Psalm 55:2-3:

> Pay attention! Answer me!
> I can't sit still while complaining.
> I'm beside myself over the enemy's noise,
> at the wicked person's racket,
> because they bring disaster on me
> and harass me furiously.

I continue in faith and walking forward by rehearsing these promises: "But I call out to God, / and the LORD will rescue me" (Psalm 55:16).

My heart is unsettled as I sit with the fact that I do, indeed, now seem to have a human enemy. But at the same time, I am in the process of being heard, saved, and rescued by others and by God. It is slow, it feels quiet, it sometimes seems like it's not even happening. But it is.

My kids see their dad every other weekend, which means that every other weekend I walk alone into church, wishing that my children could be with me. One morning, I was about to observe communion and my heart was empty without my kids sitting next to me, one on each side. I said to Jesus, "It's not supposed to be like this." I felt him say, "You're right. It's not." I replied, "Please set all things right, Jesus. Please." And he said, "I will."

Dear ones, we are being fought for in the heavenly realm. And one day, if possible sooner rather than later, let's hope we can look around our lives and proclaim that once again, we do not have any enemies.

A Prayer

"O God, the Father of all, whose Son commanded us to love our enemies: Lead them and us from prejudice to truth: deliver them and us from hatred, cruelty, and revenge; and in your good time enable us all to stand reconciled before you, through Jesus Christ our Lord. Amen." —*Book of Common Prayer*

A Next Good Step

It's moments like this when you need to round up the troops. Make sure you're sharing with a friend or two, or a counselor, about these feelings of isolation. You do not have to go through any of this alone.

A Way Forward

"If God is for us, who is against us?" (Romans 8:31)

Feeling quiet today.
And slow.

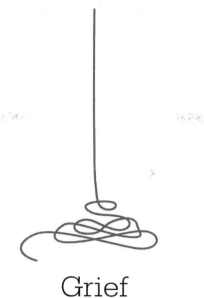

Grief

de·ca·thect (verb): to withdraw one's feelings of attachment (from a person, idea, or object), as in anticipation of a future loss.

Cathexis is the investment of mental or emotional energy in a person, an object, or an idea. So *decathexis* is the process of taking it back. The only way to do that is to grieve for what has been invested in before you can move forward. The grieving process is a mental and emotional letting go."

My marriage is over. The marriage that I hoped for since I was a little girl, the marriage that I have been a part of for so many years, the relationship that I have slaved and cried and prayed over, is finished. I am in huge pain and sometimes feel like I just may slip under the current if I'm not careful.

And yet, I know that I need to move forward. I need to grieve what I have invested so far and reclaim that emotional energy that has gone into the life, perpetuation, and now death of my marriage.

I need that energy and time back for the rest of my life to go on and then, I hope, to flourish. No matter where you believe your marriage is headed at this point, and especially if your marriage is in your rearview mirror, you must say good-bye to what was, in order to clear the ground for what is to come. Henry Cloud suggests several questions to ask yourself as part of the grieving and moving forward process. I hope my answers spur on your thinking.

"What was good about it?"

My children are the best thing that came out of this relationship. I was able to live a life that I would not have been afforded as a young single woman (mothering, a home, staying at home, a certain group of friends, starting a women's ministry, writing/speaking). Also, and most important, I depended on God so deeply throughout.

"What have you learned?"

I am very selfish. I am set in my ways. I prefer being right to being kind. I can be disrespectful to people I do not like. I overly trust but if you hurt me, I'm done with you emotionally.

I hold onto the past, to grudges, to resentments. I record-keep. I am controlling. I am harder on other's faults than I am on my own. I don't like being lonely. I don't like being told what to do. I don't like being lied to . . . I can't tolerate being lied to, actually. I am broken. But I'm stronger than I thought I was.

"Have you gained any new skills and knowledge?"

Not that I have mastered any of these things, but: How to set boundaries. How to say no. How to stand up for myself and my children. How to be a stronger mother. How to *live and let live*. How to be persistent in asking for help. How to wait. How to figure out what I need and then how to get those needs met in healthy ways. How to say *I'm sorry*. The ability to live a deeply authentic life in all my relationships. How to look people in the eye who now know the truth about me. How to not take in each comment or circumstance as a huge setback or personal affront. How to not freak out all the time.

All is not lost through this death. I have two precious children. I have learned so much. I love my friends even more now. And I'm guessing that I'm much closer to Jesus than I would've been in a solid marriage.

A Prayer

"Lord, let me return to you, let me come to you, reach out to me. I am alone. Alone. Empty-hearted. Afraid of myself. Let me come to you. Reach out to me." —a prayer from the Jewish liturgy for the Days of Awe

A Next Good Step

Spend some time asking yourself the questions above, then process your answers with a trusted friend.

A Way Forward

"I assure you that you will cry and lament, and the world will be happy. You will be sorrowful, but your sorrow will turn into joy." (John 16:20)

Relief

I have a confession to make, so pretend I'm whispering these words to you. I don't want anyone who isn't separated or divorced to hear me because they wouldn't understand:

I am completely and utterly relieved to no longer be in my marriage.

Now don't get me wrong; at the same time, I'm still devastated and bottomed out. And I know I'm not supposed to have this feeling, but I do. It was killing me, and I'm not being overdramatic when I say that. I have slept better since moving into our new home than I have in years. I feel free. I can breathe. My heart palpitations, eye twitches, and migraines have all but disappeared. Where walls were closing in constantly, I look around and see only open spaces. I can sing super loud in my kitchen. I can run through the rain and shriek with delight—without being disapproved of for shrieking too loudly. I can buy a pizza just for myself. I can order a Sprite in a restaurant without guilt. I can get what I need at Target without having to explain my purchases.

For quite a while now, I have not thrown away garbage. Now, before you picture me living in hoarding conditions, let me explain. My spouse had this thing about recycling (which is great) and composting (really great). This meant we recycled pretty much everything.

So, I find myself in my own home with my own garbage can and my own garbage disposal for the first time in my adult life, and I don't know what goes into either of them.

I text a friend, "Can I put a banana peel in the disposal?"

Almost immediately, the phone rings. "NO!"

OK, OK. So, what do I do with banana peels?

"You throw them out," she says.

I throw them out?

"Yes," she repeats. "You throw them out."

What about, like, used paper plates?

"You throw them out," she says again.

Really? I just throw this stuff out?

"Honey," she says gently, "you can throw out anything that you want to."

I can? I dance in my kitchen, listing off all the things I can throw away now.

Living in a place of inequity, especially when you didn't know that you were, drowns you. My person disappeared while I attempted to become someone different, someone better. For half of my life, I wasn't who I was supposed to be.

So now I'm learning who that person is. And I'm learning, so slowly, what is normal and what never should have been normal. The temperature on my thermostat is where I set it. And I do not have a television in my bedroom. And I take long, long showers.

No more hidden truths.

No more confusing conversations that leave me baffled.

And I'm not nervous.

And I don't cry myself to sleep.

And I don't know the last time I had a shouting match with someone in my home.

And I'm coming back to life.

I am free.

I am relieved.

And I'm throwing every single thing away that isn't nailed down. Because I can.

A Prayer

Abba Father, it wasn't supposed to be like it was. You know, I've finally woken up to the truth. I am grateful for the release, although I know it's not what you would've wanted for me and for us. Thank you that my shoulders aren't hunched anymore. Thank you that I can rest. Thank you that

I can make my own decisions—even if I mess up half of them, at least they're mine. Thank you for this freedom. Amen.

A Next Good Step

We focus a lot on what we've lost in a separation or divorce, and rightly so. But in the quietness of your own heart, can you think of a couple of things that were unhealthy, that you won't miss? Thank God for what you learned from them.

A Way Forward

"Christ has set us free for freedom. Therefore, stand firm and don't submit to the bondage of slavery again." (Galatians 5:1)

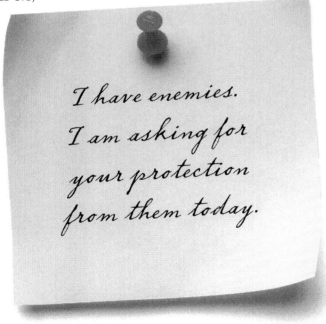

I have enemies. I am asking for your protection from them today.

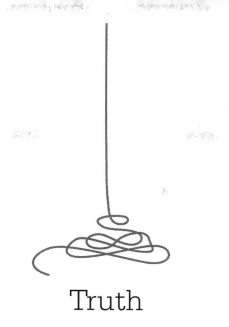

Truth

I'm a huge fan of the truth. I used to lie like a rug when I was a kid, but I've thankfully left those childish ways behind me. Many a teacher told my mom I was "creative," but I think that was their kind way of saying I lied all the time. Nothing huge, just made-up things like vacation destinations I never actually went to; saying that I'd read every assignment and then faking my way through the discussion time; and my favorite: in second grade, I supposedly had contact lenses. I milked that one for a few days.

So, I used to lie, but then I stopped.

Or did I?

Well, it depends on your definition of *lying*. My definition used to be saying something that wasn't true. But my more mature and current definition would also be *not* saying something that *is* true. And if that's the case, then I have lived most of my adult life as one big lie.

And here is that lie: that I was an emotionally healthy woman in a godly marriage with the perfect Christian family.

Lie, lie, and lie.

I am not an emotionally healthy person, although I am trying and healing.

I did not have the perfect Christian family; while my kids are amazing, I have to admit that we have broken them in some major ways. Although, God knows, not beyond repair.

But I am beginning to tell the truth. My truth. I am taking off the mask. Stripping off the labels, most of which I applied to myself and kept duct-taping back on—because God forbid that anyone could've seen what my life and marriage were really like. Then what?

I was so scared—being deeply involved in church leadership—of what might happen if anyone really knew my darkest secrets. Such as, my secret prayers that God would kill me or my then-husband because I felt I *couldn't* get a divorce.

What would people think if they found out? What would people do? Would I need to step down from leading women's ministry? from leading women's small groups? from leading mission trips? from speaking? Would I be judged? scolded? punished? shunned?

Umm, yes, to some extent. You see, at the beginning of my separation, I sent a letter to some key leaders at my church—former co-workers in some cases, former bosses in others—and told them of my marriage journey. I was terrified, but totally led by the Spirit (he does that a lot, nudges me to do things that initially terrify me).

But it's all OK. Because I've been telling the full truth for a while now, widening my tight inner circle day by day, letting people in to see all the ugliness, and you know what? Overall, the response has been kind and full of grace. Also, yes, I've stepped down from things. Yes, I've been judged. Yes, I've been scolded. Yes, I've felt punished. Yes, I've felt shunned.

But I've also felt supported and loved and seen, and above all . . . completely and utterly free. My real friends are rising to the top. My closest relationships are purer and deeper. Those who knew and loved me well before now know and love me better. And those who didn't know me well before and haven't taken the time to hear my heart, well, those are the ones who seem to be doing the judging. Funny how that all works.

Truth is spoken of throughout the Bible, touted as a high and lofty principle, one to be sought after. *Speak the truth from your heart. . . . A truthful witness saves lives. . . . Speak the truth to each other. . . . She told him the whole truth. . . . Love rejoices with the truth. . . . Set forth the truth plainly. . . . Speak the truth in love. . . . You can know the truth. . . . The truth shall set you free.*

And so I am trying to do all of these things. I'm bringing my secrets out into the light. My life is not perfect. I am striving to be a godly woman, but I am also a failing sinner who hides her true self out of fear. My marriage was broken for years and years, and it has come to an end. I hope my kids grow up to follow after Jesus with their whole hearts, but the foundation I have given them has many cracks because of my own brokenness. These are my secrets. These are the things I've been hiding from you . . . from everyone. But I'm not hiding them anymore. And do you know why? Because I want to be set free. As a dear friend once said, "Truth, good. Secrets, bad."

And you know what I'm finding? When I share my secrets, I realize that I'm not just revealing my own little story; I'm telling my part of the human story, and I'm hearing it told back to me again and again. I'm helping you to be set free, and you're helping me to be set free.

A Prayer

Holy Spirit, search my heart and dig deep under the layers of what I'm keeping from myself and what I'm even trying to keep from you. I want to live my life free and brave and in truth. Please reveal to me what is authentic and honest and real, even if it's painful for me. Amen.

A Next Good Step

Have you been keeping secrets? Maybe even from yourself? You're not fooling God, who sees deep down into your soul and knows you better than you know yourself. May I make a bold suggestion? Get out a piece of paper and begin writing down things about yourself that no one knows, things that you fear if someone found out, they might run away. Then share them with God. And then . . . share them with a trusted friend. The weight will lift off your shoulders, and you'll be surprised by the lightness that you experience. Trust me. Telling the truth matters; telling the truth heals.

A Way Forward

"Then you will know the truth, and the truth will set you free." (John 8:32)

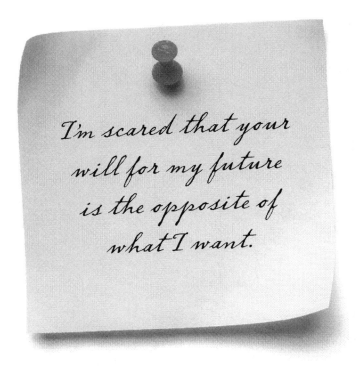

I'm scared that your will for my future is the opposite of what I want.

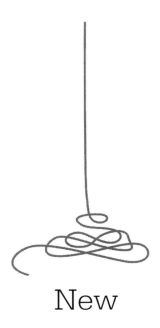

New

I am you. The details are not the same, but I hope you know by now that I understand you.

I get trying to keep a marriage together with everything that's in me.

I get praying prayers that aren't answered the way you assume they will be or should be.

I get crying yourself to sleep.

I get crying on your bathroom floor.

I get trying to maintain the image of the perfect Christian family, and how exhausting that is.

I get the shock when everything starts to unravel, when everything starts to be found out.

I get the loneliness, both in and out of marriage.

I get the sadness that comes with telling your kids their parents are getting a divorce.

I get the shame that accompanies hurtful, judging words from others.

I get the fear of not knowing what's coming.

I get the worry that you're making every single decision wrong.

I get the wondering if you're going to be alone for the rest of your life, wondering if "I'm too broken or just too much me for any man to handle."

I get feeling just slightly off, ever so slightly "less than" now that you're the d-word.

I get not being able to stop yourself from thinking you have crossed the line, and there's no way God could fully forgive you or love you anymore.

I understand you. I understand your pain.

But here's what I'm seeing: *God is a God of new things.*

I've had a few new experiences this past week. I've started attending a new church that I love, something that has taken me completely by surprise. I met my new pastor and had a wonderful conversation with him and felt so much grace and such a deep sense of welcome, exactly what my soul needed right now. My teenagers are entering new phases with drivers' licenses and mission trips and dates, and—although I'm terrified to face this alone—I *am* doing it and we'll be just fine. And I am thinking about what my next step is regarding ministry: something about advocacy for hurting women, I know that much. So there are new things in the middle of the mess and the lingering pain.

And I've been thinking about how God doesn't just make new things, although he does totally do that. He's also really amazing at making all things new. "And God will wipe away every tear from their eyes; there shall be no more death, nor sorrow, nor crying. There shall be no more pain, for the former things have passed away. Then he who sat on the throne said, 'Behold, I make all things new'" (Revelation 21:4-5 NKJV).

In other words, he's not looking at us and thinking he needs to toss us out and just start over with someone else. He is looking at us and he is dreaming up who we are going to be after all of this . . . after we make it through to the other side . . . after the struggle and the tears and the uphill battles . . . after we make amends . . . after we settle whose opinion matters . . . after we have begged for healing and joy for so long, our hearts are raw . . . after he makes us new.

"I will give them a single heart, and I will put a new spirit in them. I will remove the stony hearts from their bodies and give them hearts of flesh" (Ezekiel 11:19). We may each be struggling with different levels of anger or sadness or bitterness or fear due to our separation or divorce, or we're reeling from betrayals that have taken us by surprise or from realizing we'd been abused all along or whatever, but God is saying that he will remove our hard hearts and replace them with new hearts.

I am here to say that although it can be a long, scary process, this can happen. My primary emotion is no longer anger. My primary emotion is no longer revenge. My primary emotion is no longer fear. My primary emotion is no longer even sadness. My new primary emotions are compassion . . . gratefulness . . . peace. And if God can do that in me, dear ones, he most certainly can do a new thing in you.

A Prayer

"Dear Lord, thank you for making all my things new. For taking my sorrow and making it joy. For taking my fear and making it strength. For taking lies and making it truth. For taking my broken heart and making it whole. For taking my dread and making it hope. For taking my losses and making it service. For taking my darkness and making it glory. In the name of Jesus, Amen." —Charlotte W. Lukas

A Next Good Step

Ask yourself these questions. First, what is an old thing in your heart or life that you know God wants to work on in you? Second, if you could choose any new thing to be done in your life—dream a little—what would it be and why? Talk to God about it.

A Way Forward

Look! I'm doing a new thing;
now it sprouts up; don't you recognize it?
I'm making a way in the desert,
paths in the wilderness. (Isaiah 43:19)

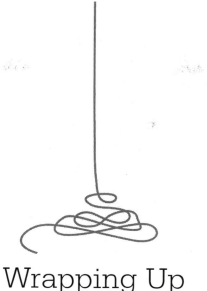

Wrapping Up

I started this book when my separation began, and I'm just now putting the finishing touches on it during the winter after my divorce. What this means for you is this: I wrote this book straight throughout my separation and entire divorce process. Not at the end, when it was all wrapped up. That means that you just got all of me—raw, vulnerable, uncensored, in the midst of my worst mess and largest pain ever. If I had waited until I had made it all the way through, my memories would be anywhere from cloudy to romanticized. And that wouldn't do you, who's in the middle as well, any good.

I wish you were sitting next to me on my couch right now, because I want to look you in the eyes so that you really hear me. I want to say that I'm so sorry. In case no one has ever said this to you through this whole experience, I am just so sorry. I am so sorry that your marriage was difficult. I am so sorry that your marriage didn't last. I am so sorry that your divorce has been painful. I am so sorry that your life hasn't gone the way you had planned. I am so sorry if anyone—even one person—has made you feel disapproved of because of your divorce. (They are wrong, by the way. *They are wrong.*) I am so sorry if you feel rejected or abandoned or unloved.

Let me offer these final words, in case I haven't made it clear. You have not irreversibly trashed your life. You are not irretrievably broken. You can and you will heal. You will not feel the way you feel right now for the rest of your life. You can trust me on this because I already do not feel the way that I felt when all this began.

Regardless of what kind of pain you might be in, you have hope. Because the Jesus that has revealed himself to me—the one who told me he loved me when I was lying on the bathroom floor . . . the one who walked me through the agonizingly difficult process of exposing my marriage and my faults in front of church leaders . . . the one who watches me as I learn what it means to be single again, to raise my children on my own—that Jesus loves me. That Jesus knows me. That Jesus sees me. That Jesus tells me that this is just one of my stories, not the final word on my life, not the thing I'm going to be known for. And that Jesus is bringing me back to life.

That Jesus is the one who is walking alongside you, too, wanting and waiting to bring a restoration out of your unraveling.

And no matter what happens to you, no matter what you choose to do . . . your heavenly Father cannot love you more and cannot love you less. I promise. And he promises.

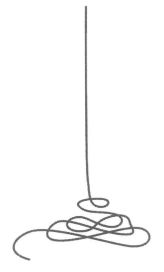

Afterword
Lauren F. Winner

Here is a list of some of the things I remembered, while I was reading Beth Corcoran's *Unraveling*:

I remembered the shame one can feel when one is a Christian, especially when one has a leadership role in church, and one's marriage is crumbling. I remembered the shame, the secrecy, and the terrible compartmentalizing—all the things you are terrified to let anyone else know, so you try not to know them yourself. It is draining and crazy-making, that kind of compartmentalization.

I remembered how kind people can be.

I remembered Jesus' relentless desire for our wholeness: Jesus' deep will that each of us be made whole.

I remembered that divorce is a serious thing, a grave thing; it is a failure, and a morally significant one.

I remembered how much pain I caused for people I cared about.

I remembered the exhaustion.

I remembered not to take for granted the pleasure of sleeping alone in a queen-sized bed.

I remembered what a relief it is to tell the truth about things.

****

I also remembered, while reading this book, that the collapse of my own marriage was the beginning of my education in grace. I had been a Christian for a decade or so when my marriage finally gave out, but I didn't really know about grace.* I didn't know what people meant when they said things like *Jesus picks up all your broken pieces and makes something better than you could have imagined, something better than before.* I thought those people were just—what? Speaking platitudes? Trying to comfort themselves? I didn't understand that they were talking about salvation, about redemption, about the *most* important things.

---

*I say "a decade or so," because how can you date the collapse of a marriage with precision?

A few years ago, I began to understand. And *Unraveling* reminded me—indeed, helped me articulate this more clearly: the way God has worked a stunning resurrection, when I thought I was going to be dead forever. It was not, as I had once hoped, the resurrection of my marriage. It was the resurrection of my soul. And it was not worked by me, or by the courts, or by the retail therapy I undertook, or even by my friends.† It was worked, is being worked, by God.

I have a friend who told me that her marriage and divorce have made her a relentless truth-teller.

I had a friend who said to me, a few years before I divorced, that he hoped I would not divorce; and then he said that if I did, he was certain that, through that experience, I would learn things about God I did not yet know. He was right.

****

Unraveling makes me think that my friend is part of a tribe, and that Elisabeth Corcoran is one of the tribes' wise leaders.

This book—as you know by now, you who are here at the end of it—is company and nourishment and courageous, relentless truth. The truth is this: in hundreds of ways, large and small, divorce underlines our brokenness; and in the midst of that brokenness, Jesus is still there alongside you, suffering when you suffer, and still moving you toward wholeness, and toward himself.‡ I am grateful for that truth, and I am grateful to Elisabeth Corcoran for telling it.

---

†Although I think those friends were often God's agents, doing a little stealth divinity.

‡Sometimes the movement seems imperceptible. It seems like a millimeter of movement. And sometimes it seems like a beautiful leap, a grand jeté.

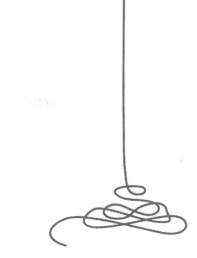

Acknowledgments

I am grateful for my children, who are full of grace as I limp, more than glide, through this most difficult season in our lives. Sara with her, "I'm proud of you," and unloading the dishwasher without being asked. Jack with his, "Is there anything I can do for you, Momma?" and, "You look like you could use a hug." I couldn't ask for two better children to be my mirrors or to hang out with. I love you both completely.

There are several key men in my life who stepped up, had my back, and continue to walk me through this. Al, Dad, Eric,

John, Mike, Tim, and the elder board of Christ Community Church. And a special thank you must go to Casey. . . . I'm not sure what I would have done without you. God provided a covering throughout this journey in the form of each of you; thank you so much for taking care of me and my children. I am also exceedingly grateful for my new church community, The Orchard. They have made me feel so welcome at a truly vulnerable time in my life.

The women in my life deserve medals for long-suffering support. I am forever indebted to my incredible girls, who have walked beside me during this dark time: Amy, Aunt Liz, Charlotte, Deb, Erika, Kate, Keely, Kelly, Jenny, Linda, Michelle, Mom, Ruthie, and Sheli. Thank you from the bottom of my soul for your friendship, prayer, and unconditional love.

A special thanks to Charlotte. . . . Who knew when I came to sit on your couch in May of 2008 what you were signing on for by taking me under your wing? Thank you for always urging me on to a fuller life and better choices, and for always pointing me right back to Jesus. These words are just a small part of your sowing in my life.

My sweet Redbud Writers Guild. I am still blown away by the blessing of being a part of this incredible community of women writers. Your encouragement is pretty much why this book didn't get tossed into my hope chest. Thank you for standing by me, standing up for me, and spurring me on.

Thank you to my agent, Blythe Daniel, for believing in me and in the message that lives don't end with divorce, and the healing of hearts matters.

Acknowledgments

Thank you to Lil Copan, Cat Hoort, Brenda Smotherman, and all the amazing people at Abingdon who helped me bring this book into the lives of hurting people.

Thank you to Lauren Winner—perhaps the biggest surprise of this entire project—who told me my book was awesome and super compelling, and then used a bunch of other words I had to look up. Grateful for your attentive eye and tender heart toward this project and toward my heart.

And Jesus . . . *oh, sweet Jesus.* How can I thank you for walking me through the water without letting me drown and for walking me through the fire without letting me get burned? Please take these words and the whole of my heart and life as a small thank you.

And Last

I want to leave you with a few resources: a final prayer, which I have prayed over my life and which you can pray for yourself as well, as often as you need to; a letter I wrote to my children, which might serve as a model for your own communication with your kids; a few additional questions to ask yourself before starting a new relationship; some gentle pointers you can give to friends who may ask how they can help you during this time; and, finally, an invitation.

Heavenly Father, I am your child, and I am hurting. I am broken. I come to you, and I picture myself climbing up into your lap. Please hold me so very close. Please help me tangibly experience your presence in intimate ways. Please show yourself to me as my healer (Jeremiah 30:17). Please restore my joy (Psalm 51:12). Please help me to release my pain to you and move forward and look ahead (Philippians 3:13). Please give me something to look forward to (2 Peter 3:13). Please use my pain to bring comfort to others who are hurting (2 Corinthians 1:3-4). Remind me that you think I am precious and that you love me completely (Isaiah 43:4). Remind me that you will always be with me, no matter what (Matthew 28:20). Amen.

Open Letter to My Children

No matter the ages of your children, keeping communication open with them is so important. I have
prayed so many times for me to be appropriately authentic with them . . . not telling them too much but also not
keeping them in the dark. This letter is something I read
to my children in the early stages of my separation, and
you can use it as a model for how to talk with your children
as well.

Dear Ones,

When I was a little girl, my parents divorced. I don't even remember them together as a couple or us as a family because I was so young.

I went on to get married, promising myself I would never, ever get a divorce. But here we are.

Your father and I are ending our marriage. We are breaking up our family. And you are in the middle of it all.

I am supposed to be stronger than you. I am supposed to be the safe one. I am supposed to be your refuge. I am supposed to be your example. But there are days when I don't have enough strength for myself, let alone for all of us.

I know this is a very difficult time in our family. I know that everything feels shaky and uncertain. And I know that you are probably feeling everything from scared to angry to wounded and betrayed by the two people you thought would protect you, let alone never hurt you. I'm sorry for failing in the one relationship that was supposed to be your model for your future. I am sorry that my weaknesses are causing you pain. I hope you'll see one day that in my choices and decisions, I've always had your best interest in mind. I am truly doing what I think is right. But I know it still hurts. A lot. (Even when you don't show it.)

But I have some good news. Some news that I did not know at your age, because I didn't yet know Jesus. Some truth that I did not know to cling to when I went through my rocky childhood.

If I could tell you anything and you would never forget it, this is what I would want you to know:

- The problems between your father and me are 0 percent your fault.
- It is not your responsibility to pick up the pieces or to make me feel better on a sad day.
- Your father loves you both completely.
- I love you both completely.
- You two and your father are a family. You two and I are a family.
- You do not have to go through this alone. More people love you, more than you know.
- You are being prayed for.
- No boyfriend or girlfriend can fill the holes in your broken heart that our broken marriage caused. Only God can.
- You are not doomed to a bad marriage. Do not be afraid to love and commit to marriage.
- Choose your husband/wife with great care.
- What is happening in our family is not a surprise to God; therefore, he is in charge.
- There is no sin and no failure that will keep you from the great love of God.
- God has said, "I will never leave you or abandon you" (Hebrews 13:5). In other words, God will always be there for you, and his love can carry you through anything.
- You're going to be OK. We are all going to be OK.

Sweet children of mine, we will be taken care of by a heavenly Father who cares about every detail of our lives and our hearts. Hold on to his hand, and he will hold you close.

All my love,
Mom

Journaling Questions Before Moving On

Here are some additional questions you can ask yourself to help process your divorce before moving on into another relationship.

1. Do I have any childhood baggage that I still haven't worked through? If so, what? How can I take steps now to process all of it?

2. Why did I choose the person I chose to marry? What did I love about him?

3. Did I see any red flags before we got married? If so, why did I choose to ignore them and push past them?

4. What did my husband do to me or how did my husband act that I now consider to be unacceptable behavior?

5. What did I do to my husband or how did I act that I now consider to be unacceptable behavior? (It goes both ways; we are not sinless.)

6. What are some ways that I can actively work on changing my flaws?

7. What did my husband do well in our marriage? Did I affirm that?

8. What did I do well in our marriage? What are some characteristics I want to enhance?

9. What steps can I be taking to heal where I am right now? (Counseling, a recovery group, finding a mentor, and so on.)

10. Have I fully grieved the losses (of either my marriage or of how I thought my marriage was going to turn out)?

11. Am I letting others into my life to speak to me truthfully about my words, actions, and thoughts?

12. What do I believe are God's next steps of healing for me, based on Scripture, what I've learned from the church, and the wise counsel around me?

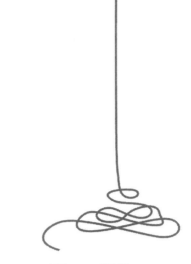

For Those
Who Want to Help

If friends ask how they can help you, you can give them this.

A dear friend e-mailed me today, "My heart hurts for you, and I wish I could do something to help you through this. Is there anything more than prayer that I can do?"

Another, "This isn't easy and no one can really make it easy for you and there is nothing I can say that will do that either . . . other than I love you, and I'm here for you no matter what."

I get this a lot. People who love me telling me they don't know how to help me right now. So, here are some thoughts if you know someone who is walking through the end of their marriage. (And frankly, most of these could be used for anyone in your life going through a hard time of any kind.)

Pray. Please. Knowing that I have people in my life who love Jesus and are talking to him about me is so huge, words almost can't express it. There are times when I can't pray, or when my prayers seem way too small or selfish, or—I hate to say it—just plain mean and immature. Having people who talk to my Savior on my behalf, in ways that I never would think of, is what gets me through this the most, hands down.

Ask us how we're doing. Caveat: but only if you can handle the truth; because depending on the day, the reply may be, "Absolutely horrible."

Check in. The occasional e-mail, text, voice mail, or note can make a person's day. This thing we're doing is isolating and scary.

Don't try to fix us or our situation. Unsolicited advice, even well-meaning, can sting and feel like we're being kicked while we're down. However, give advice freely if we ask for it, which I happen to be doing a lot, mainly because I've never walked through this before and I'm a bit clueless.

Invite. Ask us to lunch or tea. Ask our kids to do something with your family. Keep us feeling connected. We may say, "No, thank you"; but just knowing that we're included—

especially as we're transitioning out of couplehood—is essential.

Don't judge. This might be the hardest one. No one can know all the details of any situation. If you feel close enough to the person, ask the questions that you're wondering deep down, and then listen with gentleness. If you're not all that close, hand it over to Jesus. Remind yourself that we all make mistakes. In any situation there are three versions—yours, theirs, and God's. Assume the best about the person because there may be so much more to the story than you know or may ever be able to know.

Love us. Remind us that we're loved. We might be lonely. We might be beating ourselves up over pretty much every choice we've made and are making. We need to know there are people who've got our back and won't walk away. One friend said to me a while ago, "You can mess up absolutely everything in your life, and I'm not going anywhere." That's love.

Last, *show grace.* We may suck at being your friend right now. We'll get better soon, we promise. Please cut us some slack. Getting through this thing, I'm learning, is a full-time job.

Thank you, I love you, and I couldn't get through this without you.

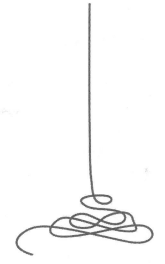

An Invitation

In the summer of 2012, I began two private Facebook groups: one for women who are in difficult Christian marriages, living out the day-to-day with their spouses; and one for Christian women who are separated or divorced, no longer living with their spouses. If you are interested in being a part of either of these growing private communities, where the women are committed to following God and encouraging each other in their difficult circumstances, please send me a message on my Facebook page (http://www.facebook.com/ElisabethKleinCorcoran), and I will gladly add you.

Blog—www.elisabethcorcoran.com/blog/
Website—www.elisabethcorcoran.com
Twitter—https://twitter.com/ekcorcoran
Facebook—www.facebook.com/ElisabethKleinCorcoran
Additional resource list for women in difficult marriages or going through divorce: www.elisabethcorcoran.com/difficult -marriage-divorce/

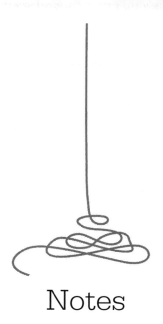

Notes

Guilt

"Lord, in your mercy," Thomas à Kempis, *A Forgiving Heart: Prayers for Blessing and Reconciliation* (Minneapolis: Augsburg Fortress, 2003).

Perseverance

"Never, ever, ever, ever," Winston Churchill, 1941, a speech at Harrow School in London.

"Beyond the cross, we," L. L. Barkat, *God in the Yard: Spiritual Practice for the Rest of Us* (T.S. Poetry Press, 2010).

"Gracious and holy Father," A Prayer of St. Benedict of Nursia (480–547), *The SPCK Book of Christian Prayer* (Society for Promoting Christian Knowledge, 2009).

Gratitude

"Accept, O Lord, our," *The Book of Common Prayer* (New York: Seabury, 1979), 836.

Children

"God our Father, you," *The Book of Common Prayer* (New York: Seabury, 1979), 829.

Loneliness

"Almighty God, whose Son," *The Book of Common Prayer* (New York: Seabury, 1979), 829.

Health

"Creator of the universe," Kathleen Fischer and Thomas Hart, *A Forgiving Heart: Prayers for Blessing and Reconciliation* (Minneapolis: Augsburg Fortress, 2003).

Fear

"All fear is but," Ann Voskamp, *One Thousand Gifts: A Dare to Live Fully Right Where You Are* (Grand Rapids: Zondervan, 2011).

"Let nothing disturb you," Prayers of St. Teresa of Avila (1515–1582), *The SPCK Book of Christian Prayer* (Society for Promoting Christian Knowledge, 2009).

Identity

"Dear God, when I," Joy Cowley, *A Forgiving Heart: Prayers for Blessing and Reconciliation* (Minneapolis: Augsburg Fortress, 2003).

Joy

"O Great Spirit of," Molly Fumia, *A Forgiving Heart: Prayers for Blessing and Reconciliation* (Minneapolis: Augsburg Fortress, 2003).

Friendship

"You have blessed us," Vienna Cobb Anderson, *Prayers of Our Hearts in Word and Action* (New York: Crossroad, 1991).

Forgiveness

"If you wait until," Dr. Ray Pritchard, *The Healing Power of Forgiveness* (Eugene: Harvest House, 2005).

"Lord, make us instruments," a prayer attributed to St. Francis of Assisi, *The Book of Common Prayer* (New York: Seabury, 1979), 833.

Hurts

"Merciful Healer, enter those," Flora Slosson Wuellner, *A Forgiving Heart: Prayers for Blessing and Reconciliation* (Minneapolis: Augsburg Fortress, 2003).

Enough

"You are being asked," Henri Nouwen, *The Inner Voice of Love* (Colorado Springs: Image Books, 1999).

"Over the years you," Nouwen, *Inner Voice*.

Anger

"O God, you have," *The Book of Common Prayer* (New York: Seabury, 1979), 824.

Healing

"I used to think," Ravi Zacharias, *Cries of the Heart* (Nashville: Thomas Nelson, 2002).

"When I got busy," *When I Got Busy, I Got Better* (AlAnon Family Groups, 1994).

"Spirit of comfort and," Janet Morley, *A Forgiving Heart: Prayers for Blessing and Reconciliation* (Minneapolis: Augsburg Fortress, 2003).

Strength

"Lord Jesus, our Saviour," Prayers of St. Augustine of Hippo (354–430), *The SPCK Book of Christian Prayer* (Society for Promoting Christian Knowledge, 2009).

Sadness

"Even the winter won't," Audrey Assad, "Even the Winter," by Audrey Assad, Bryan Edward Brown, and Mia Fieldes (Sparrow Records, 2012). Administered by BMI, ASCAP, and APRA.

Unknowns

"Spirit of Hope, blessed," author unknown, *A Forgiving Heart: Prayers for Blessing and Reconciliation* (Minneapolis: Augsburg Fortress, 2003).

Rejection

"O my Lord—wash," author unknown, *A Forgiving Heart:*

Prayers for Blessing and Reconciliation (Minneapolis: Augsburg Fortress, 2003).

Enemies

"O God, the Father," *The Book of Common Prayer* (New York: Seabury, 1979), 816.

Grief

"Cathexis is the investment," Henry Cloud, *Necessary Endings* (New York: Harper Business, 2011).

"What was good about it?" Cloud, *Necessary Endings*.

"Lord, let me return," Chaim Stern, preparatory service for the Days of Awe, *A Forgiving Heart: Prayers for Blessing and Reconciliation* (Minneapolis: Augsburg Fortress, 2003).

About the Author

Elisabeth Klein Corcoran is an author, speaks several times a month to women's groups, and is honored to be a member of Redbud Writers' Guild. During her time at Christ Community Church's Blackberry Creek Campus in Aurora, Illinois, she began and led their women's ministry for ten years prior to moving to the city's Orchard Community Church. As an outreach of her desire to help others, she has traveled to Haiti and Sierra Leone and has led a team of women to Liberia with Samaritan's Purse doing AIDS work. She pens a monthly column for moms and writes regularly for websites such as Crosswalk.com and Graceformoms.com. She lives with her children, two teenagers, in Illinois. Her idea of a great weekend would include time with her kids, time with her best friends, a bike ride, some reading, and some writing.

66680633R00145

Made in the USA
Columbia, SC
19 July 2019